Yankee Resurrection

The Wild Ride of the 1974 New York Yankees

John Bartolick

ISBN 978-0-578-63516-3

Written in memory of my Dad, my first baseball coach and my companion for many Yankee games.

Contents

Author's Note

For those of us came of age between the Ruth/Gehrig/DiMaggio/ Mantle dynasty and the Billy/Reggie era, our relationship with Yankee history is a complicated one. I was a Yankee fan by birth, and throughout my life I have recommitted to Yankee fandom by choice. Sometimes it hasn't been easy. As a small boy I found much to enjoy in the stories and memories of the Ruth, Gehrig, DiMaggio, and Mantle eras. By the time I began to follow the team, World Series appearances were a thing of the past. I did have the chance to see Mantle, Joe Pepitone, Bobby Richardson, Ellie Howard, and other Yankee stars from the 1960s both live at "The Stadium" and on television. Reverence for the names, the pinstripes, the monuments, the flags, and the majestic ballpark that bore witness to so many historic deeds made the Yankees a team like no other in sports. Yet at the same time the ineptitude, the malaise, and the irrelevance of the franchise during the period of 1965-1972 made me wonder if I would ever enjoy the exhilaration of a Yankee World Series appearance. When the day did come for my beloved team to return to the Series, I had to try hard to separate the players and their on-field expertise from the weird, almost unbelievable antics of their owner. For this and other reasons that the reader will hopefully appreciate, the 1974 season was a pivotal year in the history of the Yankee franchise. It was a season in which the impossible seemed suddenly achievable, a season in which change became a constant, a season in which the icons and assumptions of the past would be smashed in the name of progress, and a season in which the promise of franchise success once again seemed attainable. It was a year of incredible highs and unbearable lows. It was a year to say "Goodbye" to a stadium that we had grown up in, to ballplayers that we idolized, and to a management style that had left our team stagnant. It was a year to say "Hello" to a new way of doing business, to a new cast of ballplayers who were both talented and passionate about winning, and to a new sense of optimism for the present and future fortunes of "our" team.

As of this writing not one member of the 1974 team is enshrined in Cooperstown. Two of the club's most beloved players represented the team in the annual All-Star Game, but both were voted in by fans as All-Star starters despite the fact that they each were in the grips of their worst major league seasons. The owner was willing to spend huge amounts of his vast fortune to buy talent, but the rules in place at the time made it almost impossible to facilitate the acquisition of top line players with cash alone.

It was such circumstances that helped make the wild ride of the 1974 Yankees a season like no other.

Introduction

When it comes to who to thank (or, depending upon your point of view, who to blame) for the creation of 7x24x365 Sports Talk Radio, the name Art Rust Jr. needs to be prominently featured. Rust was a minor New York sports media figure, working both radio and television gigs in the New York City market for over twenty years before he joined WABC radio and launched a show called "Sportstalk" in 1981. Rust was a diehard lover of sports, but the two sports that he loved the most were boxing, a realm in which he was acknowledged as one of the greatest experts of his time, and baseball. An African-American, he specialized in the stories of great African-American athletes as they paved the way for future generations in their sports. In addition to his on air work he was a respected author and an acknowledged expert on the lives of many African-American athletes, most notably boxer Joe Louis.

Rust tapped into his great network and love of sports to create a radio talk show that was both fun and informative. Consistent with the talk radio format, listeners would call in, ask questions, share memories, spout opinions (both the informed and uninformed varieties), and, of course, argue with Rust and his guests. The show built a loyal audience, unquestionably paving the way and opening the door for New York's WFAN, which launched in 1987 as the first radio station entirely dedicated to the sports talk radio format. WFAN in turn inspired numerous other local and nationally syndicated programs and networks that copied and ultimately improved upon the original WFAN format.

On nights when Rust and his staff could not fill the air with guests they would open the phone lines for call on virtually any subject. And so it was that on one night in the mid-1980s a debate broke out amongst the callers to the show. The debate topic was a common one among fans of the New York Yankees in that era – "George M. Steinbrenner III: Good or Bad for the Yankees?" While it would be difficult to categorize those who called in favor of Steinbrenner as "fans," they all echoed a common thesis – before Steinbrenner's arrival the Yankees were boring underachievers, after Steinbrenner's arrival they were exciting and they returned to their birthright: the World Series. The pro-Steinbrenner contingent credited the club's renewed success directly to George's leadership and his checkbook. The anti-Steinbrenner crew also had a thesis – namely that Steinbrenner's meddling and mismanagement had cost the Yankees as much as it had gained and that he had made the once renowned franchise a laughing stock with his antics and with his ignorance of the game. Back and forth the two camps went. There was one caller, however, who made a point that has stayed with me for decades. Without the benefit of a transcript, his position went something like this –

"How can people say the pre-Steinbrenner era was boring? I loved those teams and I loved those players. I rooted for Bobby Murcer and Sparky Lyle and Thurman Munson and Roy White and it didn't really bother me that they didn't go to the postseason. Sure, that would have been fun. But we all cared about those guys and that's all that mattered."

To some diehard Yankee fans this may sound like sacrilege. After all, dedicated Yankee fans, raised on past Yankee glory, assume that the World Series is staged on an annual basis for their team's benefit; indeed, a trip by the Yankees to the World Series is an annual expectation. Yankee haters found this sentiment equally incomprehensible; they had spent the years in which the Yankees were in decline relishing the anguished plight of the Yankee fan, even to the point of pity. For the unfortunate fans from franchises who go decades (or even a century) without a championship, the whole topic must seem bizarre, since a relatively short absence from the Fall Classic hardly seemed to be anything to dwell on – for these unfortunate fans, the entitled attitude of some Yankee fans only adds to the long list of reasons to hate the Bronx Bombers.

It was not surprising that no conclusion was reached. The dialogue was illustrative of the divided opinions held by Yankee fans of the man that *New York Daily News* cartoonist Bill Gallo satirized as General Von Steingrabber and who others was simply referred to as "the Boss" (a moniker that represented more derision than respect). It was George Steinbrenner who had said "Enough" to those years of a lovable but mediocre team, "Enough" to what he and his newly arrived sidekick Gabe Paul called "the country club atmosphere" of the clubhouse, "Enough" to investments made without a commensurate return in the form of on-field performance and results in the standings. His arrival brought with it a culture shock, as many things changed that had been held sacred in the hearts of Yankee fans. He simultaneously embraced the Yankee tradition when it suited him and tore it down when it stood in the way of making HIS Yankee team a winner.

Yankee fans who came of age during the interregnum between the Yankee championships of the 1960s and the club's resurgence in the second half of the 1970s found themselves in a very peculiar time and place. Raised on the past and the majestic accomplishments of their favorite team, they were born into a world of tradition. Where else would monolithic monuments to past heroes be placed literally on the field of play but at Yankee Stadium? The historic stadium, the ancient clubhouse man, the iconic public address announcer, the pinstriped uniforms, the Old Timer's Days with guest lists containing the very best living ballplayers – everything about the organization oozed with reverence for the past. But in the present moment that had all seemed like some other world represented by a loving caricature. With all sincere and due respect to the fans of Cleveland and Chicago and Boston and Philadelphia and Houston and the multitude of other cities that had been deprived the joy of rooting for a perennial champion, the lean years between Yankee World Series trips hurt Yankee fans of that era with a special kind of pain, different even from that which was felt during the dry spell of 1982-1995 – at least during most of those years there had been some degree of hope and there was at least the perception that the club was overtly trying to build a winner.

The 1974 Yankees were in many ways the bridge between the lean years of the pre-Steinbrenner era and the glory years under King George in which the club won eleven American League pennants and seven world championships. 1974 was the second year of operation under the new management team, but they were the team that transformed right before the eyes of Yankee fans from also-rans to a force to be reckoned with. Along the way the Yankee faithful said farewell to people and ideas that were synonymous with the Yankees of the earlier era and accepted a new breed of Yankee who brought with them skill, personality, and that critical intangible asset – a will to do whatever it takes to win. For better or for worse, this was the start of a new era in Yankee history and a whole new period in the history of baseball.

PART 1

THE GREATEST TEAM IN SPORTS

Dynasty

The team now known as the New York Yankees was born in 1903. The fledgling American League, which had achieved major league status only two seasons before, had been blocked by the National League's New York Giants from establishing a team in New York until an agreement to plant a new franchise in the city was struck with the Giants prior to the 1903 season. The last place Baltimore Orioles were sold to a new owner, who relocated the franchise to New York. The team that established New York as their home bore no resemblance to the original Oriole club. The new team was more of what we would today call an expansion team, comprised largely of castoffs collected from established ball clubs and with only a tiny handful of players from the 1903 roster coming north from Baltimore. The club was originally called the Highlanders, an appropriate nickname reflecting the club's home location in the Washington Heights neighborhood of Manhattan. American League Park, known locally as Hilltop Park, was built to host the new team at a cost of $200,000 in 1903. Ironically, the park's left-center field power alley was almost fifty feet shallower than the corresponding section of right-center, an oddity that would be reversed in the club's future home in the Bronx. The establishment of the New York franchise was the last change in the eight team American League for the next fifty years, a period of stability that would last until the move of the St. Louis Browns to Baltimore in 1954. For the first eighteen years of their existence the New Yorkers fielded some reasonably good teams, some terrible teams, and a lot of teams in between. At the extremes, the club barely missed a league championship in 1904 and finished fifty-five games out of first place in 1912 (ironically the franchise's poorest finish ever and their last year as the Highlanders). When the Cleveland Indians captured their first American League championship in 1920 it left the Yankees, the St. Louis Browns, and the original Washington Senators as the only American League teams without a single pennant to their credit. One cannot miss the irony of the fact that it was the Yankees' most bitter rival, the Boston Red Sox, who earned the most victories in the league during New York's first seventeen seasons while also tying for the most league championships. New York's performance in the first two decades of the twentieth century offered little indication that the club would reverse course and become the century's greatest sports franchise, and a decent though unspectacular third place finish in 1919 did not seem to be a harbinger that the birth of a dynasty was about to take place.

Combined American League Standings – 1903-1919

Team	Wins	Losses	Winning %	Games Back	AL Titles
Boston	1392	1141	.541	-	5
Chicago	1385	1154	.536	10	3
Detroit	1347	1192	.523	48	4
Cleveland	1316	1230	.507	82.5	0
Philadelphia	1287	1227	.504	95.5	5
New York	**1221**	**1298**	**.477**	**164**	**0**
Washington	1113	1423	.430	280.5	0
St. Louis	1070	1466	.414	323.5	0

The fortunes of both the Yankees and the rival Red Sox were forever changed on December 26, 1919. Red Sox owner Harry Frazee was in dire financial straits. The Red Sox were but one of Frazee's many business interests, and as the year 1919 came to a close Frazee was desperate for cash. To make matters worse, his biggest baseball star was twisting his arm for a higher salary. Babe Ruth had become one of the game's rising stars, and the brash young man wanted to be paid accordingly. With the cost to keep a recalcitrant Ruth on the playing field rising in parallel with the losses and financial gaps in his business portfolio, Frazee felt compelled to sell the slugger for the cash that he so desperately needed. And so it was that the New York Yankees received one of history's greatest Christmas presents. In exchange for a series of cash installments and a rather large loan, the 24-year-old Babe Ruth became a Yankee. While Red Sox fans would not see another world championship in the 20th century, the arrival of Ruth proved to be a game-changer for the Yankees. After finishing third in Ruth's first season, the club would go on to win six of ten league championships in the 1920s, five in the 1930s, five in the 1940s, and a whopping eight out of ten in the 1950s, collecting eighteen world championships along the way. The decade of the 1960s opened on an equally successful note as the Yankees ran the American League table in the first half of the decade with a string of five league championships from 1960-1964. In recognition of the Yankees' status as the elite franchise in baseball, the Hasbro toy company created a board game called *Challenge the Yankees* in which the top stars of the American and National Leagues were pitted evenly against the Yankee roster. October baseball became a birthright to both the Yankees and their fans. Yankee fans expected their heroes to be present, if not win, every World Series. The players came to expect the annual cash bonus awarded to league and world champions, admonishing slumping teammates not to "mess with my World Series money." Club management exploited the fact that Yankee players regularly received World Series bonuses (taken from the postseason gate receipts) as leverage to get players to take lower salaries (paid directly out of the pockets of team owners), literally telling players that were unhappy with salary offers not to forget that they would invariably receive a World Series bonus. The financial impact to players traded by the Yankees to non-contenders during these halcyon days was often significant enough to convince borderline Yankee players to begrudgingly accept lower salaries in the expectation that the reduced pay would be offset by a much greater postseason bonus. It was during these decades that it was very, very good to be a Yankee and equally good to be a Yankee fan. Resentment against the Yankees and their fans grew, but the association with a perennial champion served as a wonderful benefit to offset the growing ill will.

Few benefitted more by the prestige and financial rewards of a successful New York franchise as the club's owners. The Yankees were owned by entrepreneur / National Guard Colonel Jacob Ruppert Jr. from 1915 until his death in 1939. It was during the Ruppert regime that Babe Ruth was acquired, Lou Gehrig was signed, and the lineup that became known as Murderers' Row was unleashed upon American League rivals. After Ruppert's death his estate sold the club to businessmen Larry MacPhail, Del Webb, and Dan Topping in 1945. Topping and Webb bought out MacPhail in 1947, and the franchise subsequently enjoyed its most successful run of championships with fifteen American League titles in eighteen seasons from 1947-1964. Along the way they earned a reputation for coldness and ruthless efficiency, resulting in the popular observation that "rooting for the Yankees is like rooting for General Motors," a recognition of cold-hearted success as personified by the nation's most successful (and soulless) corporate entity.

Combined American League Standings – 1920-1964

(Original American League Franchises)

Team	Wins	Losses	Winning %	Games Back	AL Titles
New York	**4292**	**2643**	**.619**	-	**29**
Cleveland	3706	3231	.534	587	3
Detroit	3571	3381	.514	729.5	4
Chicago	3413	3510	.493	873	1
Boston	3333	3595	.481	955.5	1
Washington / Minnesota	3319	3608	.479	969	3
St. Louis / Baltimore	3114	3816	.449	1175.5	1
Philadelphia / Kansas City	3076	3842	.445	1207.5	3

By 1964 there were warning signs that the ball club's fortunes were about to change. The symptoms were subtle at first. Yankee superstars like Whitey Ford, Mickey Mantle, Elston Howard, Tony Kubek, and Roger Maris, while on the whole still productive, were beginning to show signs of wear and tear. The newest cadre of stars, including Jim Bouton, Tom Tresh, Phil Linz, and Joe Pepitone, performed admirably, but despite impressive early performances none seemed destined to deliver to the level of their predecessors. The talent pool in the Yankee minor league system likewise seemed to be too shallow for comfort, with relatively few impressive prospects on the horizon. Perhaps most alarming was the rise in the quality of the competition in the league, with threats from long-time nemeses like Detroit and Cleveland compounded by the rise of perennial door mats like Baltimore, Minnesota, and Chicago to create a competitive parity in the league that had been largely absent during the Yankees glory years. Still, the club had won five American League championships in a row, and the average age of their starting lineup and starting pitching staff was twenty-eight and twenty-seven, respectively – the age of peak physical performance in that era.

Enter the Columbia Broadcasting System. By the mid-1960s CBS was looking for diversified business opportunities while it engaged in an epic high-stakes battle for American television supremacy with competitors NBC and ABC. Among the businesses acquired by CBS during this era were the famed Fender guitar company, publishing companies, educational film companies, and a tool manufacturer. In addition to this diverse range of new business ventures, the company had high hopes for acquiring a well-established and profitable sports franchise. After an unsuccessful attempt to buy a football team, the growing conglomerate re-focused its attention on acquiring the New York Yankees. CBS assigned the task of negotiating with Dan Topping and Del Webb to a rising star in their Business Development team named Michael Burke.

Parts of Michael Burke's biography read like a Hollywood movie script, so much so that even Hollywood agreed. Burke's breakthrough "role" came as a member of the Office of Strategic Services (OSS) during the Second World War. Burke's duties literally landed him behind enemy lines as a liaison between allied armed forces and units of the French resistance. Gary Cooper's character in the post war film *Cloak and Dagger* was based upon Burke's wartime experience, with Burke serving as a technical advisor on the project. Burke returned to the world of espionage with an impressive array of dangerous covert missions as an agent of the newly formed Central Intelligence Agency, the successor organization to the OSS. Burke tired of the high-risk, low-reward nature of life as a decorated CIA field agent and by the mid-1950s he was ready to move on to more financially lucrative pastures. Burke left the Agency to become Executive Director of Ringling Brothers and Barnum & Bailey Circus. Burke's stay at the circus was relatively short-lived. Dissatisfied with the fly-by-night nature of the business and the seedy characters that he was forced to deal with, Burke craved an opportunity for a more personally and financially rewarding life style. It was at this time that he became acquainted with senior members of the CBS organization, who saw in the gregarious Burke a potential that positioned him as a future leader of the CBS organization. Burke quickly entered the inner circle of CBS management, and it was an outgrowth of that series of relationships that landed him in the role of brokering the purchase of the Yankees from Topping and Webb.

Burke and CBS were almost too late – Topping and Webb had already come close to finalizing a deal to sell the franchise to a New York investment firm, but that deal fell through, clearing the path for CBS. CBS agreed to buy 80% of the Yankees at a cost of $11.2 million with an option to buy out Topping and Webb's remaining 20% for $2.8 million (CBS would later exercise the buyout option for a discounted $2 million amount, making the total purchase price $13.2 million). If $13.2 million for the greatest franchise in sports seems like a minute amount (even in 1964 dollars), consider that one day in the not-too-distant future CBS would dump the club for a mere $10 million, with an embarrassed CBS issuing a press release stating that it had "almost recouped their original investment" (translation – they lost money). Webb and Topping remained in place as limited partners, ostensibly in charge of baseball operations. The deal, still private and out of the public eye, was then submitted to the American League owners for the necessary approval. The opinions of the owners varied from ambivalence over the proposed sale to vehement objections raised by the owners of the White Sox and the Athletics. Athletics owner Charlie Finley had been an outspoken critic of anything having to do with the Yankees since his arrival on the ownership scene four years earlier, while White Sox owner Arthur Allyn argued that the sale of a franchise to a television powerhouse like CBS could undermine Major League Baseball's future broadcast rights negotiations by letting the fox into the henhouse. In the end the naysayers were voted down, and the sale was closed on November 2, 1964. In a series of events that would be repeated in less than a decade, the option to buy out Webb was exercised almost immediately, followed a year later by a similar buyout of Topping. The departure of the two limited partners cleared the path for full ownership of the Yankees by CBS, and on September 6, 1966 Michael Burke, former OSS/CIA master spy and former circus manager, was elected by the CBS Board of Directors to be the new Chairman and President of the New York Yankees.

Declinasty

Merriam Webster defines a lemon as an acidy fruit, a tree that bears said fruit, and "something (usually an automobile) that is unsatisfactory or defective." When they bought the Yankees from Del Webb and Dan Topping, CBS had bought themselves a lemon. It also did not help that Mike Burke's background as a successful master spy and circus master did not prepare him to be a successful baseball owner.

As noted earlier, the days of easy Yankee dominance of the American League were over. The club survived a scare in 1964, rising from a tight pack atop the American League standings to win the league championship by a single game over the Chicago White Sox and a mere two games over the Baltimore Orioles, a franchise that had won only a single league championship in their sixty-three year history. The Yankee players themselves realized that they were probably not the best team in the league that season and that it was their experience in playing under pressure that offset a decline in performance to secure the league title. A loss in the seventh game of the 1964 World Series resulted in the second consecutive year that the Yankees had failed to win a world championship. Horrified at this intolerable condition, the club punished first year manager Yogi Berra, removing the Yankee great for the crime of having lost control of the club during the season and replacing him with veteran baseball man Johnny Keane. Ironically, Keane had managed the Yankees opponent in the 1964 World Series, the St. Louis Cardinals. Dissatisfied with the Cardinals performance in the early months of the season, the team's brass concluded that Keane would be fired at the end of the year. Although the decision was supposed to be confidential, the team's intention to dismiss the manager at the end of the year inevitably leaked out, causing Keane to twist in the wind through the end of the season as the team conducted interviews for his successor. A miraculous finish gave the Cardinals the league pennant and the subsequent victory over the heavily favored Yankees gave them their first world championship in two decades. Pleased with the club's unlikely turnaround, Cardinal management also reversed course and Keane was offered a new contract for 1965. Embittered by the leaked reports that he was going to be terminated prior to the club's change in fortunes, Johnny Keane had other ideas. After secretly negotiating to assume the role as manager of the Yankees, Keane conferred upon his former bosses a very public embarrassment by snubbing their offer to return and announcing his defection to the enemy Yankees. It was a move that Keane would soon have great cause to regret and which arguably shortened not only his baseball career but his life.

Johnny Keane was in every way a bad fit for his role as manager of the Yankees. His personality, management style, and background were all wrong for the very unique role that he was stepping into. While Berra may have *lost* control of the team, Keane *never* had anything close to control. The newcomer failed to earn the respect of most of the club's veterans, and his reputation for petty discipline proved well-earned as he incurred the universal wrath of players both young and old by creating and enforcing a series of rules unimagined during the Yankee glory years. Perhaps none of this would have mattered if not for the more insidious fact that the injuries that had nagged veteran players the previous year became epidemic and eventually fatal to the careers of several of the club's stars. The situation was exacerbated by the fact that Keane panicked when the club's spring training performance belied the fact that the team was aging and perhaps unable to play at the level that had garnered them five straight league titles. Concerned that he might be cast as the man at the helm when the Yankees stopped winning pennants, he forced injured players into the lineups of meaningless spring training games before their injuries were healed with sometimes catastrophic consequences. As a result of this confluence of events, the first year of the reign of CBS and Johnny Keane resulted in the worst finish by a New York Yankee team in decades. The club was in eighth place on Memorial Day and remained out of pennant contention for the remainder of the season. When it was over the Yankees found themselves in sixth place in a ten-team league, a whopping twenty-five games out of first place. To further rub salt in the Yankee wounds, the league champion of 1965 was the Minnesota Twins, a club whose last franchise championship had occurred thirty-two years earlier while they were in Washington as the original Senators. In the hope that this unprecedented turn of events was a one-time occurrence, the new Yankee management returned both Keane and the same basic Yankee roster to the field for 1966 with the expectation that things could only get better. They were wrong.

1966 represented a low water mark in the long history of the New York Yankees. Continuing, and indeed accelerating, the downward spiral that had begun the year before, the Yankees began 1966 by losing sixteen of their first twenty games. With the team in tenth place and a staggering twelve games out of first place after less than a month of play, the Yankees took the first in a long series of steps to rebuild the club by firing Johnny Keane. Keane, as he feared, did go down in history as the man who led the Yankees during their fall from glory. Johnny Keane died of a heart attack less than a year later. Those who knew him well noted that the stress associated with his failed tenure as Yankee manager may well have been a contributing factor in his premature demise.

Keane's replacement was Yankee lifer Ralph Houk. After leading the team to world championships his first two seasons and an American League championship in his third year, Houk was elevated to the role of general manager after the 1963 season. Yankee management hoped that Houk could bring the former magic back to their ball club by returning to a field leadership role. That hope was misplaced. After a brief rally, the club settled into a long, losing season. When the final standings were tallied, the New York Yankees had finished tenth in a ten team league. Despite the odd statistical anomalies that the Yankees had finished in the middle of the pack both in runs scored and runs allowed (a combination that theoretically should have landed them in the middle of the standings), the club had suffered the indignity of finishing dead last. The fact that their winning percentage was higher than any previous last place team did not soothe their wounds. The situation had turned so negative so quickly that the once hated Yankees were now pitied by opposing players and fans alike.

Burke and his management team finally recognized that there was no Fountain of Youth to revitalize the aging and ailing Yankee veterans. One by one the stars of the team's glory years retired, were traded, or settled into existence as a mere shadow of their former selves. Attempts to embark upon a youth movement were thwarted by the lack of a minor league pipeline, and attempts to improve the roster through trades proved ineffective at best and counter-productive at worst. The team's statistical performance declined in 1967, though they rose a single place in the standings. The rise of the long-time rival Boston Red Sox from ninth place in 1966 to first place in 1967 only served to further demoralize the Yankees and their fans. As they watched the 1967 World Series, Yankee fans endured the painful sight of former Bronx Bombers Elston Howard and Roger Maris wearing not Yankee pinstripes but the uniforms of the Red Sox and the St. Louis Cardinals. While fans of the club tried to make the adjustment to life at the bottom of the standings, they also said "Goodbye" to most of the players who had led the club in their most recent championship run. Bobby Richardson, Whitey Ford, and Tony Kubek had retired and Clete Boyer and Phil Linz had joined Maris and Howard in new cities as a result of the ongoing rebuilding effort. Among the players who remained, Mickey Mantle, Jim Bouton, Al Downing, Tom Tresh, and Joe Pepitone had all failed to maintain the level of performance from their prime years. Age, injury, and (in the case of Pepitone) off-the-field issues had taken a toll on these once great athletes. The situation improved temporarily in 1968 when the club quietly rose to fifth place in the standings – not great, but a far sight better than the very bottom of the league. The modest optimism generated by the team's first season above the .500 mark since the championship year of 1964 was more than offset by the retirement of Mantle prior to the 1969 season. Although he had degraded physically to the point where he was just a shell of his former self, the popular Mantle had served as the team's most visible link to happier times and even at his worst the slugger remained one of New York's most potent offensive weapons. His departure left a hole in the heart of Yankee fans and a gap in the Yankee lineup. The introduction of divisional play in 1969 guaranteed the Yankees at least a sixth place finish for the years to come, but the emaciated Bronx Bombers could only muster a fifth place performance. The team's mediocrity stung fans all the more when the cross town rival Mets, long ago captors of the hearts of New York City baseball fans, captured the title of world champion in 1969, a title once assumed to be the undisputed property of the New York Yankees.

In the baseball world, the plummeting fortunes of the Yankees did not seem to taint the image of Michael Burke. The charismatic Burke had quickly established himself as a powerhouse among the owners in the American League, and when Commissioner William Eckert was fired after the 1968 season it was Burke who initially received the support of the vast majority of A.L. owners to become Eckert's successor. After a stalemate with their National League counterparts resulted in the selection of compromise candidate Bowie Kuhn to assume the vacant Commissioner's seat, the disappointed Burke settled back into the more mundane job of trying to revive the Yankees.

The seventies seemed to offer kinder prospects for the Yankees. A rebuilt minor league system was beginning to deliver talent to the club, and for once the team's limited trading practices were yielding positive results. The team leapt all the way to second place in 1970, though they were out of real pennant contention by mid-season and ended up fifteen games behind the first place Baltimore Orioles. In the days before divisional wild cards, such a finish made a return to postseason baseball seem very far away. Those prospects seemed even dimmer in the two years that followed, as the team returned to the bottom half of the standings with successive fourth place finishes.

Yankee Resurrection

While the Yankees languished on the ballfield, their fans grew numb to the pain of poor performance. For many, a trip to the World Series that was once inevitable now seemed unthinkable. Club management seemed unwilling or unable to improve the team, and the satisfactory finishes of 1968 and 1970 seemed more like the residue of luck and timing than good management. Each offseason brought the hope that the front office duo of Michael Burke and general manager Lee MacPhail might finally deliver an influx of talent that could breathe life into an increasingly stagnant franchise. Each Opening Day brought the illusion that this new season might be different. Each Fourth of July brought the realization that the Yankees were going nowhere. Even a brief flirtation with the top of the standings in 1972 seemed like a tease as the club settled back into their comfortable role as a fourth place team. There seemed to be no respite from the endless cycle from promise to disappointment. Hope began to erode as fans concluded that the club's satisfaction with mediocre performances would leave marginal players ensconced in critical roles with little hope for upgrades. Yankee fans prayed for deliverance from the monotony of the underperformance and irrelevance of a once great franchise. Few realized that their prayers were about to be answered and the club was about to embark on one of the most wild rides in the history of the game.

Declinasty

Combined American League Standings – 1965 -1973

(Original American League Franchises)

Team	Wins	Losses	Winning %	Games Back	AL Titles
Baltimore	853	590	.591	-	4
Detroit	802	650	.552	55.5	1
Minnesota	788	660	.544	67.5	1
Boston	745	706	.513	112	1
Kansas City / Oakland	742	705	.513	113	2
New York	**716**	**731**	**.495**	**139**	**0**
Chicago	701	749	.483	155.5	0
Cleveland	670	780	.462	186.5	0

Under New Management

By 1972 CBS management had realized that the foray into the ownership and operation of a baseball team had been a disaster. In the summer of that year CBS head William Paley asked Mike Burke if he would be interested in putting together a group to buy the Yankees. The offer was music to Burke's ears – he had seen the warning signs that hinted that the CBS executives might be considering divesting the club, and Burke very much wanted to remain with the Yankees, preferably as an invested owner. With his vast network of connections and the lingering appeal of the Yankee brand, he assumed it would not be difficult to find willing investment partners. He would soon find that the search for new owners would prove to be a little more difficult than he had anticipated.

One potential buyer was former San Francisco Giants manager Herman Franks. Franks had enjoyed a long first career in uniform as a baseball player, coach, and manager, most recently having managed the San Francisco Giants through four very successful seasons from 1965-1968. Franks was a rarity among his peers in that he balanced his baseball career with a wildly successful second career as a businessman. Parlaying his investments in real estate and securities into a fair-sized fortune, Franks became a business advisor to some of the game's biggest stars, including Willie Mays, Ernie Banks, and Willie McCovey. With the backing of New York financial giant Lehman Brothers, Franks and his investment partners made an offer to purchase the Yankees from CBS in the summer of 1972. Franks intended to bring Willie Mays across town from his new home with the Mets to manage the team. The Franks group came close to finalizing a deal to buy the Yankees from CBS, but the sale fell through. And while

Michael Burke would later claim that people were "falling all over themselves" to buy the team that summer, as the 1972 season drew to a close the team was still owned by the broadcast giant.

The New York Yankees were not the only baseball team in search of a new owner in 1972. Vernon Stouffer, founder of Stouffer's Frozen Foods, had obtained controlling interest in the Cleveland Indians a little less than two years after CBS had purchased the Yankees, and like CBS he had decided that it was time to sell the ball club. Indian general manager Gabe Paul engaged a group of investors headed by Ohio-based shipping executive George M. Steinbrenner III to buy the team. A native of Ohio, Steinbrenner was already a part owner of the NBA's Chicago Bulls. The Steinbrenner group was but one of many potential buyers for the team and was competing against investment groups headed by former Indians star Al Rosen, billionaire Lamar Hunt, local businessman Nick Mileti, as well as other interested buyers. It was Mileti, owner of the NBA's Cleveland Cavaliers as well as other major sport-related assets in the Cleveland area, whose offer was ultimately accepted. Rebuffed by his hometown club, the forty-two year-old Steinbrenner did not take such setbacks easily. Undaunted, he rebounded by asking Paul to find another Major League Baseball franchise that might be available for purchase. It was to that end that Paul reached out to Mike Burke and arranged an introduction that would one day lead to the sale of the Yankees by CBS to a syndicate led by Burke and the newcomer Steinbrenner.

Negotiations carried on through the remainder of the 1972 season and into the postseason. While most casual observers might consider George Steinbrenner as THE owner of the New York Yankees, the fact is that he was the largest investor among a syndicate of high rolling co-owners; Steinbrenner, along with Michael Burke, would obtain and retain title of general partner and would ultimately serve as the de facto owner (other than times in which he was suspended from the game and prohibited from running the club). Despite Steinbrenner's pronouncement that all members of the investment team were equal partners, the remaining investors were relegated to the role of limited partners, a term that caused one such partner to make the famous observation "I did not appreciate the meaning of 'limited' until I became a 'limited partner' to George Steinbrenner." The sole exception was Burke himself, who as first among equals shared the title general partner along with Steinbrenner while also holding the title of Chief Executive Officer. As CEO of the restructured franchise, Burke basked in Steinbrenner's promise that he would have unfettered control over the day-to-day operations of the ball club. Reporters declared Burke the "real winner" in the deal, a title granted in light of Burke having maintained his leadership position while also becoming a full scale partner on the ownership team, thus fulfilling his ambition to run the Yankees as an invested owner free from the reins imposed by CBS. Steinbrenner told all the world that he would keep his hands off the running of the team and leave those details to his "baseball people." Steinbrenner's announced intention to steer clear of baseball operations seemed authentic. "We plan absentee ownership. We're not going to pretend to be something we aren't. I'm a shipbuilder." Henry Steinbrenner, the new owner's father, weighed in on his son's new business venture by calling it "The only smart thing the kid's ever done." CBS was eager to enjoy the tax benefits associated with officially closing the deal during the 1972 tax year, and so with funding secured, terms agreed, and a contract of sale complete, the New York Yankees rang in the New Year of 1973 with a press conference to announce the sale of the franchise by CBS to the Steinbrenner group for a cash payment of $10 million. The attending press was shocked by the low cost of the sale, noting that four years earlier the 1969 expansion franchises, arguably the least valuable teams in the major leagues, had sold for the same amount as the fabled Yankee franchise. In addition to his promise to refrain from interfering with team operations, Steinbrenner made public his commitment to retain the key members of the Yankee leadership team, specifically manager Ralph Houk, general manager Lee MacPhail, and CEO Burke. It was a "commitment" that would be completely voided within twelve months.

The Smiling Cobra

Michael Burke's reign as the winner in the sale of the Yankees by CBS was short-lived and with the benefit of hindsight the notion that anyone other than George Steinbrenner would emerge as the winner in such a deal is tragically comical. In retrospect, it is not surprising that the storm clouds over the Steinbrenner-Burke relationship began to appear before the ink was even dry on the bill of sale. Burke, out of genuine loyalty to CBS Chairman William Paley and his other former colleagues at CBS, had echoed their company line that once write-offs and other financial magic had been applied, the sale of the Yankees had netted the broadcast giant a small profit. George Steinbrenner, uninhibited by any such loyalty, wasted no time in contradicting that point of view by publicly bragging that the purchase was "the best buy in sports" and that it was "a bargain." Paley blamed Burke for not restraining Steinbrenner, and the relationship between Burke and his beloved mentor was irreparably damaged. Still, as painful as this incident was for Burke, there were far worse troubles ahead.

Gabe Paul was a baseball lifer who could trace his roots in the game all the way back to 1920 when he took his first job in baseball as a batboy for the minor league Rochester Red Wings. From that humble beginning the energetic Paul began to work his way up the baseball front office ladder, beginning with the role of ticket salesman once he became of age. He parleyed his early connections to work his way to the front office of the Cincinnati Reds, serving first as traveling secretary and public relations chief and later assuming his first general manager role. It was while traveling secretary that his reputation as a miserly tightwad was established. It was Paul who made the grisly discovery of the body of Reds catcher Willard Hershberger in his hotel room after the player had committed suicide. Legend has it that upon witnessing the tragic sight, Paul called team owner Powell Crosley and said "I have bad news and I have good news. The bad news is Hershberger committed suicide. The good news is I recovered his meal money." Whether true or not, the apocryphal story reflects the perception that most of the people in the game had of Paul. Paul was known as The Smiling Cobra for his dual personalities – known as "a born schmoozer" with a gregarious demeanor, Paul also possessed an arsenal of ruthless tactics and a tyrannical nature. Paul's overwhelming charm could turn to a murderous attack in a heartbeat. In an era in which general managers were considered to be the cheapest and most difficult people to deal with, Paul was among the cheapest and most difficult. Enhancing Paul's reputation as one of the game's shadier characters was his campaign to stuff All-Star ballot boxes with Cincinnati Reds players while general manager of the Reds. Suspicions were raised in 1956 when five members of the Reds were among the eight players elected to start the mid-summer classic. In 1957 the Reds secured seven of the eight spots, with the great Stan Musial barely beating out a far inferior Reds first baseman. A subsequent investigation by the Commissioner's office determined that Paul had collaborated with Cincinnati newspapers to preprint ballots with the names of Reds players already filled in. With players such as Hank Aaron and Willie Mays victimized by this scheme, Commissioner Ford Frick interceded and made adjustments to the starting lineup. Baseball fans across the nation paid the price as the All-Star voting was taken away from the fans until it was finally returned with very strict ballot security to the public in 1970.

Paul left Cincinnati to run Houston's expansion franchise, but left before the new club ever played a game. He then landed as general manager in Cleveland, leading to his eventual partnership with Mr. Steinbrenner. As the sale of the Yankees to Steinbrenner's group was being finalized, Paul was dutifully fulfilling his responsibilities as Cleveland's GM. But even then all was not as it seemed.

A week after the new owners took possession of the Yankees, a press conference was scheduled to introduce the entire ownership syndicate to the public at an elite New York restaurant. During that intervening week, George Steinbrenner informed Mike Burke that three new owners would be joining the team. Among the new investors was Gabe Paul. Steinbrenner informed Burke that Paul was selling his interest in the Indians, had resigned as Indian general manager, and would be purchasing a five percent stake in the Yankees. Steinbrenner placated Burke's concerns about the arrival of Paul, whose reputation as a poisonous presence in a baseball front office was well known throughout the sport and stood in stark contrast to the style of the much more affable Burke, by couching Paul's role with the club as that of a figurehead who would enjoy the stature of partial Yankee ownership as he glided into retirement. Paul's duties would be limited to idly working on a few special projects. Knowing Paul's reputation, Burke found it hard to believe that Gabe would be content to "sit around trying to decide the age cutoff for postcard day." Burke was skeptical and more than a little suspicious, but decided to take Steinbrenner at his word. Then Gabe Paul himself disabused Burke of any notion that Paul would be a silent bystander by informing Burke that Steinbrenner had promised him the role of President of the Yankees and that he would be announced as such at the New York press conference. Apparently, Paul's idea of a "special project" was running the team. Burke, enraged by this late breaking and most unwelcomed turn of events, got Steinbrenner and Paul to agree to frame the announcement of Paul's arrival on the scene according to Steinbrenner's original "cover story" – Paul was just another limited partner with no real front office role. The savvy New York press corps was not fooled, and Mike Burke's relationship with George Steinbrenner was forever changed. Burke realized that he had been played – Steinbrenner had used him to get ownership of the club, had fed him the story that he would have autonomous control over team operations, was stringing him along regarding the role of Gabe Paul, and was now beginning the process of reneging on his promises. Things only got worse when Steinbrenner and Burke's lawyers tried to work out the details of Burke's contract with the club – it became clearer and clearer to Burke that Steinbrenner had been lying to him all along and was now pushing him out of the way. Burke's revised assessment of Steinbrenner was simple – "The man's word is worthless." Burke bluntly summarized his feelings toward Gabe Paul when he ran into Paul and his wife at a New York restaurant. When Mrs. Paul asked Burke how he was doing, Burke purportedly said "I'll be fine once I get this knife removed from my back." Just weeks after brokering one of the most significant sales in the history of sports, the winner in the deal had concluded that he could not stay on in the job he had so deeply coveted. Burke kept his decision to leave the Yankees to himself and his legal team, offsetting his rising frustration with the knowledge that future

Machiavellian efforts by Steinbrenner and Paul to push him out were a waste of energy since he was already planning to leave. Burke gained solace through private acts of resistance, such as driving Steinbrenner crazy by showing up for the official 1973 Yankee team photo wearing his "uniform" of a denim shirt, flannel pants, worn out loafers, and a mop of wavy long hair, an intentional contrast to Steinbrenner's immaculate outfit and conservative haircut. Meanwhile, Burke laid out his plans for his final weeks as Steinbrenner's partner – "George will get more and more agitated, more and more paranoid about my presence. By the time I tell him I've decided to withdraw, he'll kiss me."

Though he tried to bide his time before publicly breaking with Steinbrenner, Burke still had to conduct day-to-day operations as a member of the Steinbrenner team. The fatal break in the damaged Steinbrenner/Burke relationship came when Burke authorized a $15,000 raise for Bobby Murcer, making the player who had become the face of the Yankee franchise a member of the elite $100,000 salary club. Steinbrenner was apoplectic over the news. Any possibility of Burke maintaining a material role in the management of the team was now gone and it became clear to all concerned that Gabe Paul was now the man running the show, with Burke demoted to the role of awkward bystander. By April Burke had tendered his resignation and had agreed to reduce his role to that of a limited partner, citing his belief that his duties as redefined by Steinbrenner were too limited in scope for him to continue in an executive capacity. Steinbrenner feigned regret and asked Burke to reconsider, but Burke recognized that George Steinbrenner was not his kind of guy. Burke retained a paid role as a consultant to the Yankees and also held on to his ownership stake in the club, eventually selling his share in the team to Steinbrenner in 1981. To his lasting credit Burke was publicly magnanimous about his departure from the job he loved more than any other in his storied career, dialing down the tension with the new owner by reconciling with Steinbrenner before making his final exit.

While neither Gabe Paul nor George Steinbrenner would admit to any plan to undermine Mike Burke or Yankee GM Lee MacPhail, the personality of the two men and the course of events both before and after the announcement of Paul's arrival seem to support Burke's contention that Steinbrenner and Paul had been planning their coup from the start. Burke wasn't the only person with suspicions about the nefarious behavior of Steinbrenner and Paul. In his waning days as Cleveland's general manager, Paul had completed a trade with the Yankees that most observers had judged as lopsided in favor of New York. That trade was viewed in a whole new light when Paul's defection to the Yankees followed just a few weeks later. Cynical onlookers noted that the trade was negotiated by Paul at the same time he was undoubtedly negotiating for his own future role with the Yankees. If true, this self-dealing arrangement would be extremely unethical, and the fact that it had drawn such conjecture was a tribute to the somewhat shady reputation that attached itself to Paul. Commissioner Bowie Kuhn thought the circumstances disturbing enough to engage Paul in a discussion regarding the chain of events. Yankee loyalists Ralph Houk and Lee MacPhail defended Paul, arguing that he had driven hard to include a prized Yankee prospect in the trade and noting that the deal was but one of a flurry of deals that Paul had consummated during that period, hardly the actions of a man who had written off any commitment to the Indians future. If the Smiling Cobra had indeed crossed an ethical boundary there was no smoking gun to prove it, so the new

Yankee President moved on from the incident with one more sordid story to add to his reputation.

Yankee Resurrection

The political intrigue between Steinbrenner, Paul, and Burke was accompanied by a palpable sense of unease and turmoil in the Yankee offices. One by one, office staff and middle managers would conclude that the pleasant atmosphere of the Burke era was gone forever and it would no longer be enjoyable to remain a Yankee employee. The first front office casualty of the Steinbrenner era occurred even before Mike Burke announced that he was leaving. Howard Berk was a member of Mike Burke's inner circle. As Vice President of Administration, it was Berk's job to consult with the weather service, the grounds crew, and the umpire staff when inclement weather threatened to make the playing field unplayable before the start of a game. If the consensus opinion was that a game should not be started, Berk had the authority to postpone the game. Just three weeks into the 1973 season a torrential rainstorm hit the Bronx and Berk cancelled the game, following the accepted practice of rescheduling the game as part of a double header later in the season. Steinbrenner went ballistic when he heard of the cancellation and related financial impact of the loss of a home date, calling Berk directly and screaming "It's not raining here!!!" (Steinbrenner was 450 miles away in Ohio at the time). Berk, amazed at his treatment by a man who had promised to "stay out of the day-to-day operations of the team," concluded that he would not be able to work under such circumstances and resigned his position. It would not be long before others followed his example. Howard Berk and many other Yankee front office employees would follow Michael Burke to Madison Square Garden when Burke became President of the Garden and the New York Knicks later in the year.

A New Beginning?

The takeover of the Yankees by Steinbrenner/Paul group and Michael Burke's resulting departure caused one New York scribe to hang the moniker Cleveland Yankees on the ball club, though many fans of the team were ambivalent to what they saw as front office politics with little potential impact on the on-field product. In some ways, the shakeup was a signal that business as usual would no longer be the norm in the Bronx. Yankee fans wanted a winning team and were ambivalent to Michael Burke's "New York chic and sophistication." If the architects of a winning team were young upstart George Steinbrenner, crabby old Gabe Paul, and the rest of the Cleveland Yankees, it was fine with the average New Yorker.

George Steinbrenner was never known to be a patient man. He viewed the CBS-era Yankee management as laconic and laisse-faire, two traits that nobody could ever attach to the new owner with a straight face. In contrast, Steinbrenner was bombastic and hands-on to a fault. George Steinbrenner made it absolutely clear that he was fully committed to building a winning team and he was ready to spend as much of his (and his partners) considerable fortune to meet those ends. This was music to the ears of Yankee fans who were frustrated beyond description by the fact that the Yankee pennant machine was stuck in neutral. Unfortunately for Steinbrenner, the realities of the Major League Baseball business model restricted how he could apply his financial resources. There was nothing close to resembling free agency in 1973, with major league players shackled for life to the teams that owned the rights to them. The influx of amateur talent was also regulated by the amateur draft system, which rewarded the worst teams with the best amateur draft picks. Ironically, the draft had been initiated in 1965 partially as a measure to restrict powerhouse teams like the Yankees from stockpiling talent. A team might count on at best two or three solid future major leaguers in any given amateur draft; the Yankees generally netted only one or two and sometimes failed to secure any. The outright purchase of established players was likewise generally restricted – Major League Baseball frowned upon the practice unless it was applied at relatively low dollar values, usually as an addition to a traditional player swap or in limited straight-cash deals for lower-level and/or over-the-hill talent. If Steinbrenner's Yankees were to quickly raise the level of their talent pool they would have to do it the old fashioned way through trades, and general manager Lee MacPhail was by nature not one to be actively involved in the trade market.

Lee MacPhail had an impressive baseball pedigree. His father Larry was a pioneering baseball executive who introduced night baseball, air travel by major league teams, and significant advances in broadcasting. The elder MacPhail's resume included a short stint as part owner of the Yankees, a role that ended prematurely due to MacPhail's erratic behavior which was fueled by an addiction to alcohol. Despite his personal demons, Larry MacPhail was recognized for his contributions to the advancement of baseball with election to the Baseball Hall of Fame. Larry MacPhail paved the way for his son Lee to join the Yankee front office in 1945. Lee MacPhail remained with the club after his father's ouster, rising to the role of farm system director before leaving to take a front office role with

Baltimore. It was while with the Orioles that MacPhail rose to prominence, as the club's home grown talent combined with players acquired through a handful of very successful trades to usher in a period in which Baltimore dominated American League competition. MacPhail left Baltimore for a position in the Commissioner's office, an ill-advised detour that he corrected after two years of working for the doomed William Eckert. MacPhail returned to front office life by rejoining the Yankees as general manager after the 1966 season. It was in this role that MacPhail assisted Michael Burke and the CBS Yankees in running the ball club from 1967-1972. When MacPhail closed his career as a baseball executive he followed his father's footsteps into the Hall of Fame. All of that was of little consequence to the Cleveland Yankees; while Lee MacPhail may have been highly regarded by baseball insiders, to the new owner he was just one more part of a failed regime.

The roster of the Yankee team purchased by George Steinbrenner was filled with holes. The 1971-1972 winter trading season was one of the most active trade periods in the history of the game based upon the number of deals and the caliber of talent being exchanged. Future Hall of Famers Frank Robinson, Steve Carlton, Joe Morgan, Nolan Ryan, and Gaylord Perry, along with stars Sam McDowell, Dick Allen, Vada Pinson, Rick Monday, Ken Holtzman, George Scott, Lee May, Jim Lonborg, Jim Fregosi, Rick Wise, and Tommy John were among the high profile players dealt to new clubs. Dozens of other deals for lesser players also peppered the pages of the nation's newspapers throughout the Hot Stove League season. General managers in both leagues were clearly eager to deal. For their part, the Burke/MacPhail duo tried to fill as many of the Yankees' holes as they could in one of the most active off seasons of the CBS era.

A New Beginning?

Unfortunately, most of the players that they acquired had posted their best results in the previous decade, and the Yankees missed out on all of the aforementioned talent although they were frequently mentioned as rumored suitors for many of the marquee players who were eventually traded.

From the end of the 1971 campaign there were high expectations that the Yankees, with a surplus of right-handed starting pitching, would look to deal one of their front line starting pitchers for a desperately needed third baseman. Stan Bahnsen was the trade candidate most mentioned in the press – the right hander had posted four very solid seasons with the team, he was young, and he seemed to have potential for even greater success in the immediate future. The Yankees reportedly offered Bahnsen to the California Angels, who were at the time shopping their veteran shortstop Jim Fregosi. Fregosi had been the Angels most prominent star in the 1960s, but was now showing signs of declining performance. The Yankees were among a number of teams who thought a move to third base might enable Fregosi's production to rebound. The Angels declined a Bahnsen-for-Fregosi deal, and instead traded their declining star the New York Mets for future superstar Nolan Ryan and three other young players. That deal subsequently entered the lore of the game as one of the most lopsided trades ever made, as the move to third base did nothing to rejuvenate the fading Fregosi while Ryan thrived into what became a Hall of Fame career. In a deal that approached the Fregosi deal in terms of one-sidedness, the Yankees eventually settled on a trade that sent Bahnsen to the Chicago White Sox for infielder Rich McKinney. In contrast to Fregosi, McKinney was a virtual unknown by all but the most avid baseball fans. All of baseball, and particularly Yankee fans, were baffled by the deal. This even-up exchange seemed to make no sense for New York. Bahnsen was among the most consistent and solid young pitchers in the game and fans expected him to fetch a much higher return than a player with a single, unspectacular major league season to his credit. The strange choice of McKinney was compounded by the fact that he had no experience at third base. McKinney's sole positive attribute seemed to be that he had hit well in a small number of appearances against the Yankees. Furthermore, McKinney was also a flake endowed with a very bizarre personality. With this background, combined with a spring thumb injury and the pressure of high expectations and even higher skepticism by impatient Yankee fans, it was no surprise that McKinney flopped and by Memorial Day he was in the minor leagues. In contrast, Bahnsen won twenty-one games for his new team. Three months after the McKinney deal MacPhail redeemed himself when he acquired reliever Sparky Lyle from Boston for veteran Danny Cater and minor leaguer Mario Guerrero in what would later be recognized as one of the best deals in recent Yankee history. Despite the success of the Lyle trade, the last winter trading season of the CBS regime was viewed as a disappointment.

After the disaster of the previous winter, the 1972-1973 offseason provided much greater cause for optimism. MacPhail opened up the action by healing an open wound with the trade of McKinney and veteran pitcher Rob Gardner to the Oakland Athletics for Matty Alou. Alou was a consistently good hitter whose acquisition by Oakland late in the 1972 season helped the Athletics win the world championship as Alou was able to fill in very ably for the injured Reggie Jackson in the 1972 World Series. Alou's high salary made him expendable to A's owner Charlie Finley, but the Yankees felt that Alou's ability to get on base made him worth the investment. Finding someone to take McKinney off their hands was definitely an added bonus. But the best was still to come.

After the disaster of the last place finish of 1966, the Yankee front office concluded that a major housecleaning was in order. With a shallow farm system and few viable assets to trade, difficult choices had to be made. While there was a desire to protect franchise heroes like Mickey Mantle, rising stars like Tom Tresh and Mel Stottlemyre, and future cornerstones like Bobby Murcer, popular and productive players would need to be sacrificed. One such player tagged for new pastures was Roger Maris, whose animosity toward both Yankee management and Yankee fans had driven him to threaten retirement rather than play another year in pinstripes. Another player marked as trade bait was third baseman Clete Boyer. Boyer had been a fixture at third base for seven seasons and had developed a well-deserved reputation as one of the best fielders in the game at the hot corner. Boyer's bat may have paled in comparison to many of the other Yankee sluggers of the 1960s, but he did average fourteen home runs a year and found himself solidly in the middle of the road as far as offensive performances by third basemen in that era. Still, the Yankees publicly remarked that they could "no longer carry Clete Boyer's glove" and the popular veteran was sent to the Atlanta Braves. In a very risky move that would sadly backfire, the Yankees took a gamble by accepting rookie outfielder Bill Robinson in exchange for Boyer. The highly-touted Robinson was labeled as a five-tool superstar, the "black Mickey Mantle." All of the pressure of high expectations in the New York pressure cooker were focused on him when the 1967 season began. Not unexpectedly, the young man failed to live up to the hype and his three seasons with the Yankees turned into a nightmare. By 1970 Robinson was demoted to the minor leagues and his Yankee career was over with little to show but bad memories and unmet expectations. Given the opportunity to properly develop and play under less stressful circumstances, Robinson would eventually become a very productive player for the Pittsburgh Pirates and the Philadelphia Phillies in the 1970s. To the great frustration of Yankee fans, by the time Robinson returned to the major leagues with the Phillies in 1972 the Yankees were still searching for an able replacement for Boyer. Charley Smith, John Kennedy, Roy White, Dick Howser, Bobby Cox, Mike Ferraro, Jerry Kenney, Bobby Murcer, Danny Cater, Ron Hansen, Celerino Sanchez, Bernie Allen, Rich McKinney, and Hal Lanier were among the players who held a share of the third base duties from 1967-1972, and the hole at third base was a perennial topic of the New York Hot Stove League. To the great relief of Yankee fans, the question of third base was about to be settled with a solution that would last for the next decade.

The Yankees had long coveted Cleveland's Graig Nettles. They saw in Nettles a powerful left-handed bat with a swing designed for the short right field porch of Yankee Stadium coupled with a glove that was equal to Boyer's and was earning for Nettles a reputation as one of the best third basemen in the game. Try as they might, the club was not able to pry Nettles loose from the Twins (his original team) or from the Indians (his current employer). All of that changed on November 27, 1972 when the Yankees announced the acquisition of Nettles and backup catcher Gerry Moses for four part-time players, none of whom fit into the Yankees' long-term plans. Nettles was by far the best power hitter in a weak Indian lineup, but he had publicly battled with Cleveland manager Ken Aspromonte and the two did not even speak to each other throughout most of the 1972 season. Nettles publicly pleaded to be traded throughout the season. With rising star Buddy Bell ready to take over at third base, Nettles had clearly become expendable. Indian fans reacted to the deal in a similar manner to Yankee fan feedback on the Rich McKinney trade a year earlier, lambasting general manager Gabe Paul for trading the team's most productive and popular player in exchange for a package of unknown and part-time players. It would not be long before those same fans, as well as the Commissioner of Baseball, would smell a rat. Everyone assumed that Paul must have known that he would be jumping to the Yankees when he made the Nettles trade. Whatever validity there was to those suspicions, there was no proof and no effective remedy – the Smiling Cobra had added another chapter to his colorful biography.

The addition of Alou and Nettles, coupled with the optimistic, energetic, and highly visible new owner, generated a positive vibe regarding for the Yankees' pennant prospects for the 1973 season. This was an optimism not seen since the halcyon days of 1965. The Yankees became a trendy pick for the divisional title in the eyes of some prognosticators. The defending champion Tigers, already known as the Over the Hill Gang, seemed too old to successfully defend their divisional title. Perennial contender Baltimore was rebuilding but was almost always considered the safe bet to win the division. Cleveland and Milwaukee were considered much too thin to mount a serious challenge. The Red Sox, with an influx of new talent and an overall well-balanced team, seemed to be a serious and rapidly rising threat. Against this competitive landscape, and in light of their new additions, it was reasonable to predict that the Yankees would at least be a contender deep into the season even if they did not have the depth and quality of talent to win the division. The Yankee public relations staff relished the club's new role as potential front-runners and built a marketing campaign around the newcomers and around incumbent team stars Bobby Murcer and Thurman Munson, who were dubbed The New M&M Boys as a homage to original M&M Boys Mickey Mantle and Roger Maris. Coupled with a series of scheduled events designed to celebrate the 50th anniversary of Yankee Stadium, there was cause for optimism in the Bronx at long last.

The positive track that the team found itself on as spring training began turned into a derailment as the result of one of the most bizarre incidents in the long history of professional baseball. A salacious public scandal developed when pitcher Fritz Peterson and best friend and teammate Mike Kekich announced that they were switching families – Peterson would move in with Kekich's family and Kekich with Peterson's. In addition to drawing unwanted attention to the organization, the arrangement caused problems within the clubhouse when Kekich tried to back out of the arrangement and Peterson refused. Kekich contributed to his exile to the Yankee doghouse by getting ill and he did not appear in a game until May. Peterson was also in hot water, but at least he pitched reasonably well. It became clear that one of them had to go, and so it was that Kekich was sent to Cleveland in early June.

The regular season likewise got off to a rocky start. Steinbrenner, with expectations high and little patience for those who did not perform to his standards, was particularly ready to pounce on Bobby Murcer. Still furious for the raise awarded to Murcer, Steinbrenner was said to be on the warpath regarding the star center fielder's performance before the first game was even played. Mike Burke and others would tell the story of how Murcer cost the Yankees a win by striking out in the ninth inning on Opening Day, causing Steinbrenner to loudly and publicly deride his "$100,000 player." The story is perhaps apocryphal, since Murcer did not strike out at all on Opening Day, although he did strike out in the bottom of the eighth inning a few days later in the home opener. Burke claimed to have rebuked Steinbrenner for lashing out in public against Murcer, telling him to lay off of the team's most popular player. If that story is true, George's future track record in this regard showed that Burke's admonishment had little impact on the Boss. Perhaps more memorable than his public criticism of the team's biggest star was Steinbrenner's reaction when the players removed their caps for the National Anthem before the home opener. Horrified by the length of the hair of several players, and still a stranger to the club to the point that he could not associate names with most of his ballplayers, Steinbrenner was forced to scribble down the uniform numbers associated with the offensive heads. Those numbers made their way into a memo to Ralph Houk, along with strict orders that the offending players cut their hair, lest they find themselves on the bench or on another ball club. And so it was that the Yankee grooming code was born, and as of this writing that code remains in place. The responsibility for delivering and enforcing the owner's message fell on Houk. This was exactly the type of thing Ralph Houk resented, particularly after the club lost the game. But Steinbrenner was the Boss, and nobody understood a chain of command better than Houk. The manager dutifully read Steinbrenner's memo verbatim, uniform numbers and all. By repeating the references to numbers in lieu of names,

Houk was also simultaneously sending a message to his players that this was coming from the owner, not the manager, while also pointing a well-aimed jab at the new owner who still did not even know the names of his ballplayers. The incident was embarrassing for all involved, and it set in motion a collision course between a headstrong owner and a proud manager.

On the field, the new Bronx Bombers were performing much more like their recent predecessors than the Yankees of the team's glory years. The 1973 edition of the club began the year losing six of their first nine and ten of their first sixteen. Among the many holes in the lineup that was exposed during the first days of the season was the new role of the Designated Hitter, introduced for the first time with the beginning of the 1973 season. The new role favored teams with deep benches and an extra bat available to add to the lineup. Unfortunately, depth was something the Yankees sorely lacked, and filling the existing eight lineup spots with quality talent on a daily basis was already an unanswered challenge.

In some ways Ron Blomberg was as tailor-made for the DH role as anyone who ever played the game. A natural hitter, Blomberg was the number one pick in the entire 1967 amateur draft, a privilege earned by the Yankees on the basis of their last place finish the year before. The Yankees were so high on the outfielder that they selected him over future stars Ted Simmons, Bobby Grich, Vida Blue, Don Baylor, and Ralph Garr. The club's two previous number one picks, Bill Burbach and Jim Lyttle, went on to underwhelming professional careers. The selection of Blomberg in 1967, followed by the team's selection of Thurman Munson as their first pick in 1968, were the club's best first round picks in the first decade of the draft. Blomberg would display a formidable bat but his outfield defense proved cause for concern. Poor results against left handed pitchers during Blomberg's first two seasons with the Yankees caused Ralph Houk, already one of the strongest proponents of platooning in the game, to go to great lengths to avoid sending Blomberg to the plate against southpaws. The affable outfielder was quite confident that if he had the opportunity to face lefties more regularly he would improve his production against them, but Houk would not budge. With the absence of a true first baseman on the 1972 roster and in light of his limitations as an outfielder, Blomberg found himself as the Yankee first baseman in 1972, at least when a right hander was opposing the club. The lack of a first baseman persisted into 1973, a fact that was exacerbated by the need to also find someone to play DH on a daily basis. While the club struggled to plug the holes in the dike, manager Houk was forced to shuttle Blomberg between first base and the DH spot. It was in that latter role that Blomberg made history on April 6, 1973 as the first DH to come to the plate when he faced Boston's Luis Tiant on Opening Day. Houk employed a rotation of Blomberg, veterans Johnny Callison and Ron Swoboda, and weak hitting Celerino Sanchez at the DH spot for the first two weeks of the 1973 campaign. Of the quartet, only Blomberg provided any decent production at one of the most critical offensive spots in the lineup. The problem was finally rectified on April 17 when Lee MacPhail leveraged Mr. Steinbrenner's checkbook for the very first time to acquire veteran Jim Ray Hart from San Francisco. Like Blomberg, Hart was the quintessential DH with a solid bat and an iron glove that made him a natural for the new role. Hart rewarded the Yankees and architects of the DH role by undergoing a career resurrection at the position. Hart had been a young star with the San Francisco Giants in the mid-1960s, joining the likes of Willie Mays, Orlando Cepeda, and Willie McCovey to form the nucleus of one of the most feared lineups in baseball. Hart made an immediate impact upon joining the Giants by smashing an impressive thirty-one home runs as a rookie in 1964. After four years as one of the National League's rising stars, Hart's performance began to steadily decline. By 1973 Hart was thirty-one, overweight, and beginning to suffer the effects of a losing battle with alcohol that would shortly end his playing career. Hart was incapable of performing in the field but quite capable of swinging a productive bat. Freed from the challenge of playing in the field, Hart was sensational during his first two months with the Yankees, posting a .314 batting average through the end of May. Hart's resurgence was matched and even exceeded by Blomberg's performance at the plate. Blomberg's defensive shortcoming at first base were all but overlooked as the slugger hit .400 for the first three months of the season, gaining national attention for the Blomberg/Hart duo.

While Hart and Blomberg gave the lineup a much needed boost, the Yankee starting rotation benefitted from a very unique newcomer. George Medich was a standout on the pitcher's mound for the University of Pittsburgh. Medich's college performance earned him All-Star honors but scarce attention from professional baseball scouts. While Medich was recognized as professional baseball material, his commitment to making a career of the sport was in question, and with good reason. Medich made no secret of the fact that in addition to his desire to play professional baseball, he was equally committed to earning a medical degree and entering the medical profession. Major league teams are generally reluctant to spend a draft pick on someone who might not be committed enough to put on a baseball uniform after graduation. But Medich was persistent in his desire to balance the grueling work of achieving his medical degree with the commitment required to play professional baseball at the highest level. After corresponding with former Yankee Bobby Brown, himself living proof that a player could enjoy a productive baseball career and achieve equal or greater levels of accomplishment in the medical field, Medich made his case to the scouts. Enough doubt remained that Medich was still available when the Yankees selected him in the 30th round of the 1970 draft as the 700th overall pick in that draft. Medich rewarded the team's confidence by progressing steadily through the minor league system, earning a role in the Yankee starting rotation in 1973. Tagged with the predictable nickname of Doc, Medich became the team's most consistent starter, eventually finishing third in the Rookie of the Year voting at season's end.

By early June the club had shaken off the early season doldrums and was enjoying a 40-24 run which landed them in first place on June 9. As a harbinger of the future and in fulfillment of the dreams of long-suffering Yankee fans, Mr. Steinbrenner's "baseball people" orchestrated the acquisition of two marquee pitchers on June 7. Steinbrenner wrote another large check to acquire the service of Sam McDowell from the San Francisco Giants. Only a few seasons before McDowell had been the most feared left handed pitcher in the American League. Premature physical decline fueled by alcohol abuse had diminished McDowell's performance to the point that he was banished by the Cleveland Indians to the Giants in a blockbuster trade prior to the 1972 season. After a mediocre season and a half in San Francisco McDowell found himself wearing pinstripes. On that same day the Yankees sent another check and three minor league players to the Atlanta Braves for pitcher Pat Dobson. Like McDowell, Dobson had an impressive resume on the pitcher's mound. Unlike McDowell, whose physical presence and overwhelming fastball earned him a reputation as one of the game's premier power pitchers, Dobson thrived on guts and guile. Though somewhat underwhelming physically, Dobson delivered excellent pitching performances in Detroit, San Diego, and Baltimore. As recently as 1971 Dobson had won twenty games with the Orioles as part of their history-making starting rotation that featured four twenty game winners. Dobson followed that performance with an All-Star season in 1972, but still found himself on the move again, this time to Atlanta. A poor start in Atlanta earned him a ticket to the Yankees, his fifth club in five years.

Yankee fans were thrilled with the acquisition of two potential first-tier pitchers. McDowell and Dobson added instant depth to the starting rotation, and their acquisition provided further evidence that the club was now in the control of someone committed to winning and willing to pay whatever price necessary to secure a championship. With estimates that the two new acquisitions cost the Yankees over $200,000 in cash plus the low-level minor leaguers surrendered for Dobson, the new owner was indeed putting his money where his mouth was. McDowell and Dobson both began their Yankee careers with very effective pitching performances, and by the traditional midway point of July 4 the team found themselves in the driver's seat atop the American League eastern division, four games ahead of Baltimore. With a solid and suddenly deeper pitching staff, Ron Blomberg hitting a remarkable .396, and stagnant competition offered by the rest of the division, postseason baseball seemed to be in the immediate future for the Yankees. The club held on to the first place slot into early August and absorbed a brief slump to remain in contention through most of the month. It was at that point that the team fell apart completely. Neither Hart nor Blomberg were able to maintain their blistering batting paces, and ace reliever Sparky Lyle fell upon hard times with just eleven appearances and a 1-3 record over the last two months of the season. The lack of depth and all of the holes in the roster seemed to be exposed during this period. Even the newly reinforced pitching staff could not prevent the ball club that had started out the season with such great optimism from ending the season by losing twenty-four of their last thirty-six games. Faced with the city's wild response to an improbable run to the World Series by the cross-town rival New York Mets, Yankee fans seemed to sense that the canary in the coal mine was dying and largely abandoned hope for the club well before the Yankees were mathematically eliminated from the pennant race. After their tantalizing run at the top of the standings through most of the season, the 1973 Yankees would go on to finish a shocking seventeen games out of first place. To add insult to injury the club finished in fourth place, unable to improve upon their place in the standings from the two prior years.

Yankee fans had witnessed a partial rebirth of their beloved franchise and had experienced the dedication of the new owner to deliver a winner. They had also begun to recognize the new owner's obsession with winning and intolerance for the sin of losing. When King George explained his role as an absentee owner who would delegate responsibility for his team's performance to his baseball people, he set himself up in a perfectly insulated position. He could take the credit for the good things that happened (like laying out the cash to acquire two quality starting pitchers), while creating a cast of subordinates who were conveniently available to blame for any failures that might occur. It was in this scenario that the meltdown of the Yankees during the critical last weeks of the season was unforgivable in the eyes of George Steinbrenner, and someone (other than the owner) was going to have to pay the price of failure.

The Major

Perhaps the most amazing feature of Ralph Houk's major league career was how little time he actually got to step onto the playing field. Houk's place in history as one of the most prolific bench warmers was not a result of a lack of talent, but poor timing and poor placement. After three impressive seasons in the Yankee minor league system, Houk's career was derailed by a four-year stint in the U.S. Army at the height of World War II. Houk applied for and was accepted to Officer's Candidate School, and upon graduation was commissioned as an officer in the Ninth Armored Division and sent to the battlefields of France. Houk distinguished himself in combat, earning Bronze and Silver Stars as well as a Purple Heart in some of the most deadly battles of the war. The death of his unit's senior officers in the Battle of the Bulge left Second Lieutenant Ralph Houk in command. Houk received a battlefield promotion to First Lieutenant, followed by two subsequent promotions, leaving the service at the end of the war with the rank of Major. To say that Houk's military service would mold his leadership style would be an understatement. Ralph Houk learned to care for his men and did not easily tolerate anyone who would interfere with his leadership.

At the age of twenty-six, Ralph Houk returned to the Yankees after four years away from baseball. Houk was fortunate that his baseball skills had not diminished, and after a year in the minors Houk joined the Yankees as a backup to starting catcher Aron Robinson in 1947. Joining Houk in a backup role was another returning serviceman named Yogi Berra. Five years younger than Houk and possessive of a much more powerful and highly coveted left-handed bat, Berra leapt ahead of Houk and took over as the club's starting catcher in 1949. Thus, Ralph Houk had the misfortune of playing catcher for a team that now featured Yogi Berra ensconced behind the plate. In addition to being one of the greatest players to ever play the position, Berra was also durable and relatively injury-free during Houk's prime years. To make matters worse, Houk was the number three man on the Yankee catching depth chart, ranking behind number two catcher Charlie Silvera. After three years of splitting playing time between the Yankees and the minor leagues, Houk finally stuck with the club in 1950. Over the next three full seasons Houk's playing time was limited to a TOTAL of twenty-two games, twenty-one trips to the plate, and just four hits. So rare were the opportunities for Houk to swing a bat that the novelty of his first hit of 1953, which occurred well into the season, drew mention in the *Sporting News*. By this time Houk was thirty-three and his days as a major league player were numbered. In August of 1953 the Yankees promoted twenty-two year-old rookie catcher Gus Triandos to the major league club and released Houk to clear room for the newcomer on the roster. Recognizing Houk's talent as an astute student of the game, the Yankees immediately signed him as a coach. Houk was reactivated as the third-string catcher again in 1954, and he was again released and re-signed as a full-time coach and bullpen catcher in midseason after logging a single at bat during three months of riding the bench. With this final release from the active roster Ralph Houk's career as a major league player was over but a new, more successful career had begun.

Houk's apprenticeship under manager Casey Stengel and coach Bill Dickey during his time with the Yankee ball club served him well. Soaking up wisdom from these two elder statesmen, Houk was dubbed "The Answer Man" by his teammates. The Yankees recognized his potential and gave him the opportunity to gain managerial experience in the highly regarded Yankee minor league system. Houk returned to the big club as a coach in 1958, and within a year was being mentioned as a likely successor to the aging Stengel. Yankee stars, who had chafed under Stengel's abrasive treatment, fueled these speculations with a whisper campaign against their veteran manager, spreading stories about the aging Stengel's drinking habits and suggesting that he was out of touch and was relying more and more on Houk to conduct the daily operations of the club. This campaign increased when the heavily favored Yankees lost the 1960 World Series to the underdog Pittsburgh Pirates, leading to the forced retirement of Stengel. Ralph Houk was named as his replacement. Ironically, Yogi Berra was among the veteran star players that Houk inherited.

Houk immediately made his mark on the ball club. In stark contrast to Casey Stengel, Houk quickly earned what would be a lifelong reputation as a player's manager, one who earned and maintained the respect of his ballplayers while maintaining a necessary level of discipline and control. Many of Houk's former players would go on to speak reverently of Houk decades after his departure from the Yankees.

On the field, Houk's Yankees were in the midst of an historic run of success. Both the 1961 and 1962 Yankees won world championships, and the 1963 Yankees crushed their competition to win an American League championship before losing to the Los Angeles Dodgers in the World Series. After Houk's wildly successful three-year managerial run, Yankee management decided that the Major deserved another promotion, this time from field manager to general manager. His successor in the managerial role would be none other than Yogi Berra.

Houk's reign as general manager was not nearly as successful as his managerial career. To his credit, his acquisition of veteran pitcher Pedro Ramos in the waning days of the 1964 season is often cited as one of the turning points that allowed the Yankees to barely win that year's league championship. Beyond that the period was noteworthy only as the starting point for the decline of the organization. In the wake of Houk's move to the front office, the Yankee players never adjusted to having former teammate Yogi Berra as their manager. Yogi never fully gained control over a team of former peers with extremely strong personalities, and Houk was faced with the horribly unpleasant task of firing the lovable Yankee legend after just one season as manager. While both Berra and Houk had made the leap to managing players with whom they had played alongside, the two men were worlds apart in their leadership styles. While both possessed astronomical baseball IQs, Houk was a man who garnered instant respect from his former teammates while Berra could never shake his clownish image and his role as one of the boys. Berra's replacement, Johnny Keane, likewise failed to earn the team's respect and support. After the team took a nosedive under Keane, Houk was asked to return to the field as manager in May of 1966 and revive a ball club whose spirit was broken and which sat at the bottom of the standings. Houk's magic worked only to the extent that the attitude of the club markedly improved – the Yankees were the most content last place team in sports. Houk continued as a fixture in the Yankee dugout for the next six years, largely unencumbered by oversight or interference from the front office. All of that was about to change.

The Major

Despite his early promise to the contrary, George Steinbrenner was never a man who was going to defer to his "baseball people" and leave his hands off the day-to-day operations of the Yankees. Ralph Houk felt Steinbrenner's searing glare on his shoulders, and he didn't like it. Protective of his players to a fault, Houk particularly resented Steinbrenner's public criticism of team members. Steinbrenner fancied himself a sportsman, having played college football at Williams College and later serving as an assistant football coach at Northwestern and Purdue. This of course added nothing to the new owner's credentials or knowledge regarding baseball. Steinbrenner's ignorance of the game and of baseball personnel only added to the frustration caused by his public commentary. Steinbrenner himself made things worse with observations like the one he made after the Yankees acquired Pat Dobson in mid-1973 – "We needed a left hander and we got one" (the rest of the entire baseball world knew that Dobson was right handed). Evidence that Steinbrenner's influence was fueling resentment in Houk came in mid-August when the club sold infielder Bernie Allen to Montreal in the middle of the pennant race. As mindful as anyone of a chain of command and previously loathe to show a break in the ranks, Houk assured Allen that "neither he nor Lee (referring to general manager Lee MacPhail) had anything to do with this." As an ironhanded disciplinarian by nature, Steinbrenner was the antithesis of Houk and was aghast at his manager's reluctance to publicly criticize or discipline his players. No event illustrated this dichotomy better than the infamous "hot dog incident" that occurred in Texas in mid-August during the heat of the pennant race and at the time the Yankees began to melt down. Reserve infielder Hal Lanier, with special awareness of fellow infielder Gene Michael's phobia of cold, slimy objects, placed a raw hot dog in Michael's glove while the team was at bat. As Michael trotted out to his position he felt the cold frank in one of the glove's fingers and freaked out, pulling the hot dog from the mitt and throwing it near the field box where Mr. Steinbrenner was sitting. The Yankee bench roared with laughter, but the Boss was horrified, later claiming that "in the heat of a pennant race Michael was more concerned about who put a hot dog in his glove than playing the game." Steinbrenner called on Houk to identify and punish the culprit, but Houk had more important things to worry about and ignored the owner's orders. The relationship between owner and manager deteriorated further during that same series when George Steinbrenner exhibited his trademark anger and pettiness, this time directed at veteran Johnny Callison. Callison had made an out during an important at bat in the prior series, and in Texas he misplayed a base hit in the outfield after entering the game in the eighth inning as a defensive substitute. Steinbrenner allegedly decreed "I will not have 'that man' on my ball club" and ordered that Callison be cut from the squad (perhaps it was a coincidence, but Yankee players noted that Callison was among those who laughed loudest at Gene Michael's reaction to the hot dog in his glove, a fact perhaps known by the owner). At first Houk refused to comply, but GM Lee MacPhail convinced Houk that he had no choice and Callison was gone. The fact that neither Allen nor Callison had been performing well was overshadowed by the fact that after a decade of significant influence over the front office, Ralph Houk was now clearly out of the loop on personnel decisions and he did not like it one bit.

The ball club was not performing well, and many of Steinbrenner's criticisms, though harsh and inappropriately aired in public, were not far from the mark. Houk believed that the psyche of the ballplayers and the independence of the field manager were essential to good performance (Hall of Fame Manager Tom Lasorda once summarized the concept by referencing the dairy industry's marketing tagline "Contented cows give better milk"), but these two factors weighed little on the mind of George Steinbrenner. The Yankee collapse in the last weeks of the 1973 season, fueled by the public criticism by Steinbrenner, resulted in Yankee fans turning on the once popular Houk. Rumblings of dissatisfaction with Houk began growing in the stands of Yankee Stadium and on the streets of New York. Fans paraded a banner through the empty rows of seats at Yankee Stadium imploring Steinbrenner to "Fire Houk!" While this was an act that would have been unheard of a season before, it summarized the simmering frustration of a fan base that had been promised a winner and that was looking for a scapegoat when that promise was not kept. With stories of George Steinbrenner's impatience and unprecedented turnover in the Yankee front office, speculation about the impending dismissal of Ralph Houk became commonplace. The proud ex-soldier was not about to suffer the indignity of being fired. After the last game of the 1973 season Houk cheated his executioner and announced that he was quitting. A manager with Houk's reputation and track record was in high demand and his absence from the game would be short-lived. Within two weeks of his departure from the only organization he had ever worked for, Ralph Houk signed on as the new manager of the Detroit Tigers.

PART 2

HOME AWAY FROM HOME

The Second Choice

One of more noteworthy trivia items of the Yankee dynasty was the fact that for forty-three of the forty-four years from 1918-1960 the Yankees were managed by Hall of Fame managers, including Miller Huggins (1918-1929), Joe McCarthy (1931-1946), Bucky Harris (1947-1948), and Casey Stengel (1949-1960). The extended period of success naturally generated relatively little turnover at the managerial position. Huggins died while owning the manager's seat, McCarthy resigned due to health reasons, and Stengel was forced out his job largely due to his age. This period of stability came to an end with the departure of Stengel, and the Yankees absorbed four managerial changes in the decade of the sixties. Ralph Houk's second tour as Yankee Manager from 1966-1973 may not have yielded any trophies, but at least it had been a stable time. All of that was about to change.

The coup against Houk was generally unpopular with the players, but public commentary by Yankee management, both past and present, was mixed. George Steinbrenner allegedly asked Houk to reconsider and remain in his role, but even if true the sincerity of that request could reasonably be questioned. Steinbrenner made a similar claim about requesting Michael Burke to stay after the latter announced that he was leaving the organization, but it was clear that Steinbrenner and Burke were incompatible and destined to part ways. The tactic of removing someone from their role and finding a soft landing for them somewhere else in the organization was one that the Boss would employ frequently throughout his ownership reign. In later years Steinbrenner would make a point of bragging that that many of the managers that he had fired were still employed by the team in other roles, implying that he was not an overbearing bully but rather a magnanimous steward of his employees' careers. Burke himself teased the headline that the Yankees had considered firing Houk and replacing him with Billy Martin during periods in which Martin was unemployed following managerial stints with the Twins and the Tigers. Indeed, the specter of an unemployed Martin would loom over Yankee managers until Martin's death in 1989, with Billy always seeming to be a phone call away from a turn in the Yankee manager's seat. But at the time of Houk's resignation Martin had settled in to a brand new position as manager of the Texas Rangers, and while that relationship would come to a predictably unpleasant and untimely end like every other managerial job that he held, for the time being Billy Martin was not available for the Yankee job. (Ironically, Houk would go on to be Martin's successor as manager in Detroit). Despite the purported attempt by George Steinbrenner to reconcile with Houk, Houk's mind was made up and he and his former employer finalized the financial and legal terms of his departure, ending Ralph Houk's thirty-four year association with the New York Yankees.

Houk's resignation spared Steinbrenner the potential public relations fallout associated with firing Houk (something he cared little about) and the necessity of paying Houk a severance package (something he cared very much about). It also presented the opportunity to fill the manager position with a Steinbrenner/Paul guy, someone from the outside who could help break the status quo in the clubhouse and shake up the action in the dugout and on the field. Throughout his reign, Steinbrenner would consistently lean toward dynamic, outspoken, well-known managers with established track records of success. This would be his first opportunity to employ this tactic and secure a marquee name to manage his club. And he knew just who he wanted.

Like Ralph Houk, it did not take Dick Williams long to achieve success as a major league manager. Williams grabbed the attention of the baseball world when he led his Impossible Dream Red Sox from a ninth place finish in the season prior to his arrival to an American League championship during his rookie managerial season of 1967. Unfortunately, the prickly Williams did not enjoy an effective relationship with Red Sox owner Tom Yawkey or the Red Sox players. Williams followed his championship season with two more winning seasons but was nonetheless fired in the waning days of the 1969 season. After coaching for a season with the Montreal Expos, Williams returned to the managerial ranks as the manager of the Oakland Athletics in 1971. In Oakland, Williams showed that his success with the Red Sox was no fluke. In three seasons with Williams at the helm, Oakland won a divisional title in 1971 and back-to-back world championships in 1972-1973.

In addition to leading a team to the World Series in his first season as a big league manager, Williams had two additional things in common with Houk – he did not easily tolerate a meddling owner and he worked for one of the most meddlesome owners in the game. Prior to Williams no manager had survived two full seasons under A's owner Charlie Finley. Williams's predecessors, Hank Bauer and John McNamara, had both led the team to second place finishes and McNamara had won eighty-nine games. The win totals under both McNamara and Bauer were higher than any Athletics team since 1932. Nevertheless, they each found themselves out a job. Williams's ability to survive three full seasons was a tribute to the fact that the Athletics won their division each of those years and to Williams's ability to balance the joy of managing a champion against the sheer frustration of working for Finley. By the conclusion of that third season the frustration had outweighed the joy to the point that Williams decided enough was enough. Before the pivotal seventh game of the 1973 World Series he told his ballplayers and his owner that he would not be back in 1974. Finley acknowledged the upcoming departure of Williams during an awkward exchange between the two men on national television during the clubhouse celebration after the A's clinched their second straight title. With a brusque "Even though you're not going to be with us next year, I want to thank you for the great job you've done for the three years you've been with me," it seemed like the Oakland Athletics chapter of Dick Williams's baseball career, and his connection with Charlie Finley, were over.

The sudden and relatively unexpected availability of Dick Williams in the managerial marketplace immediately caught the attention of George Steinbrenner, as the astute Charlie Finley knew it would. Steinbrenner had resolved to have the best of everything for his Yankees, and Williams had achieved the stature as one of the very best managers in the game. There was a serious complication in any aspiration that Steinbrenner had in regard to Williams – when Dick Williams walked away from his job he also walked away from a legally binding, multi-year contract. Finley could not force Williams to return to manage his team, but he could prevent him from managing anywhere else. And that was just what Finley resolved to do. Just two days after the public breakup between Finley and Williams, Finley announced to George Steinbrenner and to the world that Williams remained under contract with the Athletics and that any attempt by the Yankees to sign Williams in any capacity would be viewed as tampering and would therefore be subject to legal action. Williams expressed shock and disbelief that Finley would refuse to release him from his contract, assuming that jumping from his contract would "not be a big deal." Finley was adamant, playing the role of victim to the hilt. "When a manager gets fired," Finley said, "He makes damn sure he gets paid for how many years he has left on his contract. Well, now the shoe is on the other foot, and I'm left holding the contract." And in a nod to the impending Christmas season, Finley noted "My name isn't Santa Claus. I can say very emphatically that it is Charles O. Finley, not St. Nick."

Finley had both contract law and baseball precedent on his side. During his managerial days, American League President Joe Cronin had his contract bought out by another team so that Cronin would be free to manage his new club. More recently, the New York Mets had given the Washington Senators a significant sum of money (over the years the amount would be reported to be between $50,000 and $250,000) and major league pitcher Bill Denehy in return for the rights to bring Senators manager Gil Hodges home to New York to manage the Mets. The Yankees recognized that Finley was playing a very strong hand and attempted to develop a compensation package that would induce Finley to release Williams. Charlie Finley was a businessman, always ready to make a deal that might benefit him and his club. He would therefore be pleased to release Williams from his contract, provided the Williams's potential new employer recognized his magnanimity with compensation appropriate for a manager of Williams's stature. Finley concluded that if the manager of a losing team like the Senators was worth Bill Denehy and a very large check, the manager of a two-time world champion would be worth much, much more. The Yankees reportedly offered $150,000 and two unidentified minor league prospects. Finley rejected the offer as inadequate and countered with a demand for Thurman Munson, later lowering his demand to top Yankee prospects plus the cash payment. Yankee counter-offers included the likes of Horace Clarke, Ron Swoboda, Tom Buskey, and Larry Gowell. With the two sides at an impasse and unable to reach an agreement, Steinbrenner tested Finley's resolve and signed Williams to be the new Yankee manager on December 18, 1973, without any compensation to the Athletics. A Yankee jersey was hastily procured and a celebratory photo of a jubilant Williams wearing the iconic pinstripe shirt was released to the world. Dick Williams was subsequently introduced to the press and the public as the new Yankee manager at a lavish press gathering. The Yankees had their man – that was, until Charlie Finley made good on his threat to use all means at his disposal to block the hiring of Williams.

Finley filed a grievance with the American League office and a lawsuit in the United States District Court. The Yankees responded by filing a similar challenge against the Detroit Tigers for signing Ralph Houk, who had also walked out in the middle of a contract. Outgoing league President Joe Cronin conducted an extensive hearing on both matters, receiving hours of testimony from involved parties including Williams and Houk. In the end he sided against the Yankees in the Williams case, binding Williams to the Athletics for the duration of his contract unless Finley released him, and against the Yankees in the Houk case, freeing Houk to manage the Tigers without compensation. As an explanation for these two seemingly contradictory resolutions, Cronin focused on the interactions between the outgoing managers and their owners. In Houk's case, the Yankees and Houk collaborated on a press release and the Yankee front office ended Houk's profit-sharing plan with the club, effectively terminating his employment. The implication was that if the Yankees had wanted compensation from anyone for signing Houk they had missed their chance, opting instead to wait two weeks and even then not objecting until Finley had blocked them from signing Williams. In the case of the Athletics, the televised discussion between Finley and Williams during the World Series celebration was not considered an agreement by the team to terminate Williams. Cronin also gave weight to an argument that Houk had signed his contract with one owner (CBS) and resigned from a different owner (Steinbrenner). A few weeks later a judge also sided with Finley. Dick Williams's tenure with the Yankees was over before it even began. A gloating Finley announced that he would consider making Williams available to manage any club – except the New York Yankees. Williams would begin the 1974 season on the sidelines, biding his time in the real estate business while his name was floated as a potential replacement for almost every managerial vacancy and every time a major league manager fell on difficult times.

Precious time had been lost as the Yankees pursued Dick Williams. As the date for the opening of the spring training camp grew closer, the criticality of filling the open managerial position increased. A manager and his staff need time to prepare for spring training, and time was running out. Most top tier candidates were by this time employed elsewhere, limiting Yankee options. With just seven weeks left before the start of spring training the Yankees announced that they had given up on getting Williams and signed their next choice, former Pittsburgh Pirate

Manager Bill Virdon. Steinbrenner, who continued to hold out hope that Williams would become available, initially tried to veto the hiring of Virdon, but after a face-to-face meeting with the candidate he relented and Virdon was hired on January 3. For his part Virdon was well aware that he was not the Yankees preferred selection, a fact that was hammered home all too clearly in a proposed contract clause that stipulated that if and when Williams became available he would become the new manager and Virdon would be demoted to the role of coach with a commensurate cut in pay. Virdon agreed to the terms with the stipulation that his pay would remain the same even if he was subsequently demoted.

Like Williams, Virdon met the desired qualifications for the job. Virdon was a hardnosed task-master, someone who would shake up the laissez-faire attitude of the "country club." He was an outsider whose passing interactions with the Yankee organization were limited to playing in the Yankee minor league system in the early 1950s and playing against the Yankees in the 1960 World Series. He also had a track record of success as a manager, albeit a slightly more limited record than that of Williams or even Ralph Houk. After proving his ability to run a club at the minor league level, Virdon apprenticed as a big league coach with the Pirates. As a key member of Danny Murtaugh's coaching staff in 1971, Virdon assisted in the rise of the underdog Pirates to an unexpected world title. Upon Murtaugh's retirement for health reasons following the 1971 World Series, Virdon was handed the managerial reigns. He led the Pirates to a first place finish in his rookie season, losing a five-game League Championship Series to the Reds. With the Pirates having won three divisional titles in the last three seasons, Virdon's team was favored to easily win a fourth title in a weak National League eastern division in

1973. From the start of the new year things went horribly wrong. The problems began with the tragic death of Pirate legend Roberto Clemente on New Year's Eve. The loss of the star left a hole in the lineup and in the clubhouse. Virdon's plan to replace the late Clemente in right field with catcher Manny Sanguillen proved to be a mistake and that experiment was ended in mid-June with the Pirates in fifth place. Ace pitcher Steve Blass suddenly lost the ability to throw strikes, resulting in one of the most legendary declines in performance in baseball history. While the Pirates hovered around the .500 mark into early September, they were fortunate that none of the other clubs in the division were performing much better and the team was still in the championship contention as part of a five-team pennant race. On September 6 the club's underwhelming performance and a series of public feuds between Virdon and Pirate players resulted in Virdon's removal as manager with the club tied for second place with a 67-69 record, three games behind the division-leading Cardinals. The baseball world was shocked that a team would make such a major move in the middle of an intense pennant race, but the Pirates believed that returning Virdon's more experienced predecessor Danny Murtaugh to the dugout might provide the extra edge the team needed to secure a divisional title. Ironically, Murtaugh did no better than Virdon. Virdon was not unemployed long and was hired to manage Houston's AAA Denver Bears for the 1974 season prior to receiving the offer to manage the Yankees. As a professional courtesy Denver released Virdon from his contract (without compensation) and Virdon was free to play his part as George Steinbrenner's man in the clubhouse with the specific mission to shake up the team.

Yankee Resurrection

It is traditionally the privilege of the manager to select his coaching staff. Exceptions are made in some cases for organizational fixtures to be retained regardless of managerial changes – legendary Yankee third base coach Frankie Crosetti remained in his role from 1946-1968 under managers Joe McCarthy, Bill Dickey, Johnny Neun, Bucky Harris, Casey Stengel, Ralph Houk, Yogi Berra, and Johnny Keane. Crosetti's successor, Dick Howser, had become another one of those fixtures, embedding himself in the Yankee third base coach's box after Crosetti's departure from the team prior to the 1969 season. Widely heralded as an outstanding asset with a future as a big league manager, Howser was not going anywhere. First base coach Elston Howard was also well entrenched on the coaching staff and was likewise not to be impacted by the change in skippers. Like Howser, Howard was tied to the Yankee organization, and was rumored to be a longshot candidate for the manager's job prior to the hiring of Virdon. The Yankees were committed to Howard maintaining a visible role in pinstripes. Jim Turner, Ralph Houk's seventy year-old pitching coach, used Houk's departure as an opportunity to retire after fifty years in the game. It was George Steinbrenner and Gabe Paul who would choose Turner's replacement, not Virdon. The management team turned to another Yankee legend to handle the pitching staff, luring Whitey Ford out of retirement to handle the duties of pitching coach. That left Bill Virdon with only a single coaching slot to fill with one of "his guys" – the role of bullpen coach that was vacated when incumbent Jim Hegan followed Ralph Houk to Detroit. Not unexpectedly, Virdon hired Mel Wright to be his bullpen coach and his close confidant as he moved into this new and unfamiliar territory. Wright had served as pitching coach under Virdon in Pittsburgh and was under contract to fill the same position for Virdon in Denver for the 1974 season. Like Virdon, Wright relied on the goodwill of the Denver owners to release him from his contract once the opportunity to follow the skipper to New York arose. Wright would loyally follow Virdon wherever Virdon's managerial journey would take him, serving as a coach under Virdon in Houston and Montreal and remaining by Virdon's side until Wright's death in 1983.

As a postscript to the bizarre Williams/Virdon saga, Dick Williams was released at midseason by Finley so that he could take over as manager of the California Angels. As a tweak to George Steinbrenner and the Yankees, Finley publicly claimed that Williams had been released without compensation as a gesture of friendship to Angel's owner Gene Autry. There is some evidence that this was not entirely true and that a rather large sum of money had privately changed hands. In any event, Bill Virdon was able to eventually go about his business without having to look over his shoulder for Dick Williams. Avoiding the specter of George Steinbrenner would be quite a different story.

Shopping List

One of the key attributes of the declinasty years of the Yankees was the club's unspectacular track record when it came time to upgrade the roster through trades in the off season. By the early 1970s whatever core the club had was derived through their minor league system, and even the best farm system is generally not able to supply all of the talent necessary to build a sustainable, winning program.

The Yankees made very minor roster changes after the 1964 and 1965 seasons. They followed this by an extensive house-cleaning after their last place finish in 1966, parting company with Elston Howard, Clete Boyer, Roger Maris, and Pedro Ramos and getting very little value in return. The club would not make another major trade until December of 1969, when problem child Joe Pepitone was shipped to Houston. Even in that instance the player received, former Yankee prospect Curt Blefary, proved to be a major disappointment who lasted barely more than a year with the team. The club largely stood idle again until the winter of 1971-1972 when they made headlines with the Stan Bahnsen for Rich McKinney debacle, following that deal with the acquisition of a few second string veterans whose best years were behind them. Fortunately they did not give up and on March 22, 1972 they traded veteran Danny Cater for the relatively unknown Sparky Lyle. Lyle blossomed in New York, and almost made fans forget the unmade and the one-sided trades of the Yankee front office. The new regime's acquisition of Graig Nettles and Matty Alou prior to the 1973 season demonstrated that the Yankees would no longer act as bystanders during the Hot Stove League. As the club prepared for the 1974 season the determination to upgrade the roster was stronger than ever.

The final management link to the CBS era was severed at the end of 1973 with the departure of general manager Lee MacPhail. Though the Yankee decline had already begun prior to MacPhail's arrival as GM in 1966, the malaise that characterized the remainder of the CBS era was at least in part a reflection of MacPhail's personality and leadership style. Although MacPhail left under good terms (he was ostensibly leaving to take the position of President of the American League upon the retirement of Joe Cronin) his departure was inevitable. MacPhail was a conservative general manager, lacking the boldness that would mark the Steinbrenner era. He believed that winning teams were built by good scouting and patient player development. He explained his philosophy by stating "I don't believe it is possible to build a winning team by trades. It is a must to develop your own players for the key spots, then possibly fill in here and there by trading. I feel our program of development is coming along and will eventually pay off." This statement is the polar opposite of the philosophy of both Gabe Paul and George Steinbrenner, and it is inconceivable that MacPhail would have lasted much longer as general manager given Steinbrenner's legendary lack of patience and Paul's obsession with making trades, not to mention the fact that MacPhail's approach was not paying the expected dividends. Like Houk, MacPhail acknowledged that change in ownership had marked the beginning of the end of his time with the Yankees. In another similarity to Houk, MacPhail was well liked by the New York sportswriter community. The New York

Yankee Resurrection

Chapter of the Baseball Writers Association made MacPhail and Houk their guests of honor at their 1974 banquet. MacPhail marked the occasion by reading a self-written poem entitled "The Perils of Ralph and Lee or Whatever Became of Our Five-Year Plan?" The piece was simultaneously self-effacing, reflective, and a little bizarre – in short, an excellent summary of MacPhail's tenure in office. MacPhail's observations included:

(In reference to his inaugural year as GM in 1967):

"Our big move for that initial season.

Put Mantle on first, for some damn reason."

(Regarding the disastrous Bahnsen-for-McKinney trade in 1972):

"Somehow with nary a sigh or a whinny,

We traded Stan Bahnsen for Rich McKinney."

(Referring to the arrival of George Steinbrenner on the heels of the acquisition of Matty Alou and Graig Nettles and the subsequent optimism for 1973):

"Well, the first thing to happen to change the tenor,

was the sale of the club to George Steinbrenner.

Now I don't mean to imply that's necessarily bad.

But it sure as hell is not what we had."

Other "highlights" memorialized in MacPhail's tome included the 1968 doubleheader in which position players Gene Michael and Rocky Colavito were pressed into service as pitchers, Bernie Allen's three home runs in a 1972 exhibition game, the Peterson/Kekich family swap, and the time Yankee second baseman Horace Clarke was gifted a car in his native Virgin Islands despite the fact that he did not know how to drive.

For the Yankees, MacPhail's move to the American League office had the dual benefit of placing a potential Yankee ally in the league president's chair and clearing the last major remnant of the CBS years from the front office. It was MacPhail's predecessor, Joe Cronin, who had sided with Charlie Finley against the Yankees in the Dick Williams affair and with the Tigers when they signed Ralph Houk without compensation. MacPhail made it quite clear that had he been league president he would have ruled differently on both matters. While the matter was closed and therefore beyond MacPhail's control as he assumed the presidency of the league, his position on the situation was music to George Steinbrenner's ears. With the departure of MacPhail, the stage was now set for Gabe Paul to increase his direct involvement in activities regarding personnel. It was Paul who would take on the task of procuring new talent. Paul, known as one of the most prolific (though not one of the most successful) traders in the game during his time running the Reds and the Indians, was well connected, possessed boundless energy, and had a clear mandate from his boss/partner to build a winning team at virtually any cost.

Winning teams require high-quality talent and chemistry. In the eyes of Steinbrenner and company, the talent level needed to increase and the chemistry of the club needed to be shaken up. The Steinbrenner front office had three weapons in their arsenal that their predecessors lacked and which would prove essential to their desire to rapidly rebuild the club – a willingness to make changes, a shrewd and well connected general manager with an insatiable appetite for making deals, and an owner with deep pockets who was willing to spend whatever it took to field the best lineup possible. The latter weapon would prove difficult to wield in the era just before the changes in free agency rules prior to 1977. In 1974 the use of cash to procure talent was limited to mid-tier players and supporting role players. Though the options for acquiring players in straight cash deals were limited, the cash-for-players market was the theater of operations that the Steinbrenner/Paul team focused on when flexing their financial muscle in the 1973-1974 off season.

The Yankee wish list for the winter of 1973-1974 was a long one. The team had addressed one of the revolving doors at their corner infield positions by acquiring third baseman Graig Nettles a year earlier – now it was time to address first base. The team's weakness up the middle also needed attention, as mediocre offensive and defensive production from second base and shortstop had been a glaring and unaddressed issue for many years. The team also needed a right fielder, preferably one who hit from the right side to platoon with Ron Blomberg. In late 1973 the Yankees had thinned the ranks of an already depleted outfield by parting company with veterans Johnny Callison, Ron Swoboda, Felipe Alou, and Matty Alou. A backup catcher and insurance for Jim Ray Hart at the right handed DH spot were also on the list of proposed upgrades.

Shopping List

The club began to fill their shopping cart at the annual baseball winter meetings in December. In a move that illustrated the team's sincere desire to upgrade the middle infield, the first acquisition of the winter was that of Texas shortstop Jim Mason. The cost for Mason was 100,000 of George Steinbrenner's dollars, the first of many, many times that the Steinbrenner regime would overpay in order to ensure the acquisition of desired talent. Mason was an odd choice as the first piece in a rebuilding program. Acknowledged as not much more than an above-average fielder, Mason's offensive production was almost non-existent. Still, he had two attributes that made him appealing for the job. First, his name was not Gene Michael. The second attribute was best articulated by the aforementioned Michael himself. When assessing the man who had just been handed his job, Michael remarked "Well, at least he *looks* like a shortstop."

A day later the Yankees made two more moves that would have a more significant impact on the upcoming season. Steinbrenner again used his financial power to pry a player loose from the cash-strapped Texas Rangers. This time it was utility player Bill Sudakis, who came at the much more reasonable price of $35,000. Sudakis could switch-hit, provide some power at first base and the designated hitter slot, and if necessary serve as an emergency catcher, a position that he had played before a set of bad knees had limited him to other parts of the field. But the real prize won on that day came courtesy of a trade with the Kansas City Royals for outfielder Lou Piniella.

Piniella's nomadic journey to New York was rather strange, even in the crazy world of baseball. Piniella had a reputation for a bristling personality that inevitably grated on the nerves of managers and front offices alike. Seattle Pilots teammate Jim Bouton characterized the baseball community's perception of young Lou Piniella in his book *Ball Four* with the observation "Lou Piniella has the red ass," baseball slang for someone who seems to have gotten out of bed on the wrong side every single morning. Since signing with the Cleveland Indians in 1962, Piniella had been an employee of the Washington Senators, the Baltimore Orioles, the Cleveland Indians (again), the Seattle Pilots (for one spring), and finally the Royals. Topps Trading Card Company recognized outstanding young prospects each year by featuring them on special rookie cards in their annual card sets. Piniella's face graced an unprecedented four rookie cards for Washington, Baltimore, Cleveland, and Seattle before he finally found a home in Kansas City. Along the way Piniella had battled and burned bridges with managers at an alarming rate. In one of the defining moments of his minor league career, red-assed Lou Piniella fell into the realm of equally red-assed manager Earl Weaver. Still many years from establishing his reputation as one of history's most volatile (and successful) managers, Weaver had already adopted the persona of no-nonsense task master when young Lou Piniella joined his Elmira Pioneers in 1965. It did not take long for these two fiery-tempered individuals to lock into mortal combat. Berated, fined, and ultimately suspended, Piniella eventually came to accept the level of discipline and the passion for winning that Weaver had modeled; at the time, however, he was far from appreciative. The animosity between the two lasted well beyond their single year together, and even when Piniella established himself as a star at the major league level Weaver would continuously taunt the outfielder about his fielding skills. Ironically, Weaver's hectoring of Piniella over his glove work would again take center stage before the 1974 season would be over.

As hard as Weaver was on the young outfielder, he had eventually come to believe that Piniella had a future with the organization. The Oriole brass had other ideas, and Piniella was shipped to the Cleveland Indians. As damaging as the hothead tag was to the career of a young player, it was while with the Indians organization that Piniella had also earned another label with even more career-killing potential – AAA player. This unwelcomed classification denotes someone who is good enough to excel at the highest levels of the minor leagues but lacking in some crucial element necessary to translate minor league success into a career in the big leagues. Indeed, Piniella's career had been stalled at the AAA level in the Indian organization. Forced to spend three full seasons in Cleveland's Portland affiliate, including a short-lived attempt to make Piniella a catcher, Piniella held up his part with .289, .308, and .317 seasons from 1966-1968. Piniella's inability to crack a weak Cleveland lineup with that level of performance was a sign that he had no future with the Indians, a fact made even clearer when he was left unprotected in the 1968 expansion draft. The Seattle Pilots invested $175,000 in Piniella by making him their seventeenth pick in that draft, but by the end of the spring of 1969 Seattle management had formed a poor opinion of Piniella and the outfielder found himself yet again close to another year in minor league oblivion. A reprieve in the form of a last minute trade to the expansion Kansas City Royals saved him and served as the turning point in his baseball career. Piniella made the most of his new found opportunity, and at the end of that season he was crowned the American League Rookie of the Year.

Yankee Resurrection

In addition to his legendary temper, Lou Piniella developed a reputation for inconsistent performance, interleaving .300 seasons with sub-par years. 1973 had been one of those sub-par seasons, as Piniella finished with a .250 batting average, a sixty point drop from the previous year. The perception of declining performance, his proximity to the age of thirty, and the emergence of right handed hitting outfielder Jim Wohlford had convinced the Royals that Piniella was excess baggage to be used as trade bait. The Yankees, on the other hand, saw a fiery competitor who was an elite hitter and who had suffered a run of bad luck. To acquire Piniella, the Yankees tapped into one of their greatest strengths – right-handed pitching. Despite a 12-6 record in 1973, reliever Lindy McDaniel was viewed as an expendable player who at thirty-eight did not have many productive seasons left. To the Royals, McDaniel seemed to fit their immediate need to shore up their thin bullpen. So eager were the Royals to make the deal for McDaniel that they threw in pitcher Ken Wright in addition to Piniella. McDaniel would win just a single game for the Royals in 1974, and would be out of baseball following the 1975 season. Meanwhile, Piniella embraced his move to New York. Though uncertain of his role with his new club, Piniella vowed to do "whatever the Yankees wanted." It was that approach that made Piniella an immediate fan favorite, a status that he would enjoy for the rest of his career in New York. Perceptive Yankee fans saw that red ass as the mark of someone with a deep passion for personal and team success.

Even as the Hot Stove season ended and the club reported to spring training, Gabe Paul was not done wheeling and dealing. Over a four day period during spring training the Yankees rounded out their roster with the acquisition of right hand hitting outfielders Walter Williams and Elliott Maddox.

Walt Williams was a solid player, known for his hustling ways and an effervescent personality that made him a both a fan favorite and a popular addition to the clubhouse. After making a brief debut with the Houston Colt .45s at the age of twenty in 1964, Williams followed a circuitous route that led him to the outfield of the Chicago White Sox in 1967. Williams stood only five and a half feet tall, but he was stocky and lightning quick. He gave the White Sox six productive seasons, peaking in 1969 when he finished sixth in the American League in hitting. Williams was exiled to Cleveland after a contract dispute and once again performed well in a semi-regular role. He was not pleased with his ticket to New York. While he had been limited to a part time role with the Indians, Williams saw the potential for even less playing time with the Yankees. Paul's shopping spree had populated an outfield that had several more bodies than positions available, and Williams saw himself at the bottom of a long and still growing outfield depth chart. He would need that effervescent personality to keep him from slipping into a funk caused by too much time on the bench if he was to be ready to step up when and if the opportunity to prove his worth came up.

Maddox was an enigma, a young player with an outstanding glove and seemingly unlimited potential who had seen his career stalled at previous stops in Detroit and Washington. Drafted out of high school by the Houston Astros in the fourth round of the 1966 amateur draft, Maddox chose instead to attend the University of Michigan. It was from there that

Detroit drafted him in 1968. After a brief but successful minor league career, Maddox joined the Tigers in 1970. The next four years would prove to be an extremely frustrating time for the youngster. A series of injuries, a trade from Detroit to Washington, and a revolving door of managers would combine for a chaotic distraction for Maddox. Whenever Maddox would begin to settle in and establish himself as a solid major league performer, something would happen to set him back. Chief among these hurdles was Billy Martin, who made no secret of his dislike for Maddox during the times that they briefly overlapped with the Tigers and the Texas Rangers. In both cases Maddox found himself on the receiving end of a deal shipping him elsewhere, and the hand of Billy Martin was clearly visible both times. It was Martin who had buried Maddox on the Ranger bench in the spring of 1974, and Maddox recognized that the inevitable deal that sent him to the Yankees was a great opportunity for a fresh start. Maddox arrived at Yankee camp with an unimpressive .239 lifetime batting average but a reputation as a first class outfielder. As a former center fielder renowned for his own glove work, Virdon appreciated the defensive upgrade offered by the presence of Maddox. Still, with Roy White and Bobby Murcer seemingly entrenched in left and center field, and with Maddox's reputation for a sub-par bat, it was hard to see where, if anywhere, he might fit in. That question became even more intriguing in the days following the arrival of Maddox as chatter about Maddox's defensive abilities led to a consensus opinion that he might be the best outfielder on the Yankee roster, an assessment that soon morphed into the suggestion that he was the best *center fielder* on the Yankee roster. It was this latter point that proved the most controversial, since center field was the unquestioned realm of Bobby Murcer. Manager Bill Virdon added fuel to the fire in response to a reporter's question about whether or not Maddox, with his superior glove, might loosen Murcer's grip on the center field job. "If Maddox hits and proves he's a better center fielder I wouldn't hesitate to move Murcer," said Virdon. Asked whether Murcer would accept such a move, the manager gave the quintessential Bill Virdon answer – "Let me worry about that," further illustrating that the new skipper's attitude was very, very different than his predecessor when it came to his attitude toward his ballplayer's feelings.

With just twenty-five spots on the major league roster, the Yankees needed to clear roster space for the newly acquired players and for the taxi squad of stockpiled talent like Fred Stanley and Rick Dempsey. Veterans Hal Lanier, Jerry Moses, and Wayne Granger were all traded or released. The release of Granger near the end of spring training was the biggest surprise, as the others had either performed poorly in the previous season and/or had already been replaced. In the case of Granger, the departure of McDaniel had left the club a bit short of experienced right handed relievers, and Granger still seemed to have some effective years left in his arm. A nasty contract dispute had rendered Granger persona non grata, and he was released during the last of the spring cuts. Promising youngster Tom Buskey won Granger's spot in the Yankee bullpen in support of Sparky Lyle.

True to form, Gabe Paul had been a prolific trader, but he had been unsuccessful in negotiating a blockbuster deal of the magnitude that would move the Yankees into instant contender status. Despite his collection of right hand hitting outfielders and the purchase of a promising shortstop,

Paul had been unsuccessful in securing a first or second baseman. Still, he had continued to demonstrate that he was willing to do whatever was necessary to upgrade the team, and nobody thought the Yankees were done dealing.

Spring

Like any manager, Bill Virdon had his faults. Organizing and running a spring training camp was not one of them.

Virdon had a number of priorities as he prepared his team for the 1974 season. The men who hired him made it clear that the "country club attitude" that permeated the team had to change. The no-nonsense style of Virdon was perfectly suited for this task, a trait that helped turn George Steinbrenner from a Virdon skeptic to a Virdon supporter once the two finally met. The next task was to mesh the roster of players handed to him by Gabe Paul into an effective unit, filling in remaining holes as effectively as possible until Paul could bring in reinforcements. Finally, the club would need to perfect the fundamental skills necessary to be a winner. That meant drills – lots and lots and lots of drills. And drills were Bill Virdon's bailiwick.

Virdon meticulously planned every minute of spring camp life. Optimizing the use of space and time, Virdon developed a rigorous schedule of drills and conditioning. A strong believer in physical fitness and at a relatively young age of forty-three, Virdon was ready to lead by example when it came to whipping his new ball club into shape to start the season. Veteran players and spring training coaches were aghast at the intensity of the training regimen. In contrast, previous Yankee camps during the dynasty years had been known as low-key affairs. Players used the time to work on their tans, carouse, play golf, and slowly work their way into shape for the season. The natural ability of many of those players compensated for their laid back attitude toward regular season preparation

– when the bell rang, those great Yankee teams were always ready. The 1974 Yankees had no such superstars, and the club would need to function as a tight unit from game one in order to compensate. Mickey Mantle, a veteran of the Houk regime as a player and now a guest instructor in the new Yankee spring camp, noted that "Virdon was working those outfielders hard. I was getting sick just watching them." Virdon's program would pay huge dividends, particularly with a dramatic improvement in the outfield defense displayed by the club as the season progressed.

With the month of March halfway behind them, the Yankees were missing one very important face. With so many holes to fill, the last thing the Yankees needed was to create a new one. Sparky Lyle had proven just how closely the team's fortunes were tied to his own performance during the disastrous 1973 season. When Lyle performed at the top of his game, the team rode the top of the standings. When Lyle declined later in the season, the team's performance plummeted. Rather than recognizing that their bullpen ace was essential to the club's pennant hopes, Steinbrenner and Paul chose to alienate the reliever by playing hardball during his salary negotiations. Focusing on Lyle's decline in the final two months of the season, the Yankees refused Lyle's demand for a $10,000 raise for the 1974 season. As the impasse between owner and player dragged on, Lyle missed the beginning of spring training. At this point the club exercised a relatively new option to automatically renew Lyle's 1973 contract for the 1974 season. The ramification of this action, which was a relatively new addition to the basic agreement between Major League Baseball and the player's union, was unclear at the time. Major League Baseball Players Association leaders believed that any player who played a full season under such an automatic contract renewal would be eligible for free agency the following year, but that theory had never been tested. Lyle, for his part, maintained that he was not interested in free agency and that he just wanted what he considered to be fair compensation consistent with his stature as one of the game's best relief pitchers and to his value to the Yankees. The contract dispute would drag on all year, with Lyle finally signing a contract on the final day of the 1974 season that gave him a retroactive $7,500 raise for 1974 season and another raise for the 1975 season. With that future outcome still far from certain, Lyle's status with the club during the spring of 1974 was tenuous. Lyle was extraordinarily popular with fans and teammates and there was nobody on the pitching staff even remotely capable of filling his shoes. Still, owners often overlook such factors in the midst of bitter contract discussions and often do vindictive and even stupid things to punish or rid themselves of players who would not bend to their wishes. Throughout the offseason and into the spring Lyle's name surfaced in trade rumors, including the never-ending rumors of a trade with the White Sox that would bring shortstop Bucky Dent to the club. All that aside, Sparky Lyle was now in camp and would soon be prepared to resume his spot as the cornerstone of the Yankee bullpen.

As spring training wound down, owner George Steinbrenner decided it was time to address head on an elephant in the room that had been festering since the previous October. If there was a popularity contest held in the Yankee clubhouse pitting current owner George Steinbrenner against former manager Ralph Houk, Houk would win by acclimation. Houk's loyal former players harbored a continuing resentment against Steinbrenner for his interference with Houk's management of the team and for what they saw as the owner's influence in hastening Houk's departure. That same resentment could not help but taint new manager Bill Virdon.

Yankee Resurrection

Yankee players were still expressing their bitterness toward their owner by dropping anonymous quotes to the press. It was an unhealthy situation and something needed to be done to clear the air. The owner first met privately with Sparky Lyle. Lyle was known to be a frequent clubhouse critic of the owner, and Steinbrenner had likewise been unrestrained in his criticism of the team's ace reliever. The two resolved their immediate differences, and Lyle admitted to being one of the players quoted in recent derogatory news stories that painted Steinbrenner as a meddlesome distraction who knew nothing about baseball. With the reconciliation between Lyle and Steinbrenner completed for the time being, Steinbrenner addressed the assembled players and staff in Fort Lauderdale the next day. Sparky Lyle was among the most enthusiastic voices in response to the owner's speech. While acknowledging the perspective that he was far more directly involved in the day-to-day activities of the club than he had initially promised, Steinbrenner emphasized that his hands-on style was simply a reflection of his passion for winning. Steinbrenner's performance on that day was a huge success, greeted by sincere and spontaneous applause by the team. A state of détente had been achieved, if only for a while.

Gabe Paul continued his efforts to upgrade the roster throughout the spring and into the new season. In fact, Paul's frequent player transactions earned him a new nickname from cynical Yankee players, who dubbed the club President "Dial-a-Deal." Paul's proclivity for making deals notwithstanding, there comes a time when the music stops and twenty-five chairs need to be filled to start the season. With the arrival of

Opening Day, half of the players selected to go north with the club had not been on the roster at the start of the previous season. Of the twenty-five players who had been on the Yankee roster for George Steinbrenner's first Opening Day as Yankee owner, only eight would be in pinstripes when the 1974 season ended.

With the defending champion Baltimore Orioles looking very strong, a Boston Red Sox roster that featured a talented mix of veterans and rising stars, and the inability of Gabe Paul to fill the remaining gaps in the lineup, the prospects for a Yankee resurgence in 1974 were bleak when the club broke spring camp and headed north to start the season. In stark contrast to the beginning of the 1973 season, the optimism surrounding the revitalized club and the new ownership and management team was replaced by a mixture of pessimistic and realism. Yankee beat writer Phil Pepe summed up the opinion of many prognosticators with his preseason prediction for the 1974 team – "Third place; disappointing last year and improvement, if any, is negligible."

Shea

The New York Yankees were not complete strangers to the idea of playing their home games in someone else's ballpark. The franchise's first home park was Hilltop Park in New York's Washington Heights (thus the original nickname Highlanders). The club's entry into the community created a natural rivalry with the New York Giants, a rivalry that took a back seat in 1911 when the Giants' beloved Polo Grounds burned down and the Highlanders offered their home park as a temporary residence for the Giants while they rebuilt their own ballpark. The Giants returned the favor a year later, offering the Highlanders the opportunity to leverage the brand new and more spacious Polo Grounds IV for select home dates in 1912. By 1913 the two teams agreed to a more extensive and formal arrangement, making the Polo Grounds the new home park of the newly rechristened New York Yankees.

The cozy relations between owner and tenant chilled over the ensuing nine years. The arrival of Babe Ruth and his fifty-four home runs in 1920 electrified New York baseball fans, and soon the Yankees were outdrawing their landlord. Apart from the indignity associated with this turn of events, it had become clear to Yankee owner Jacob Rupert that it was more than time for a new stadium for his club, one suitable for the throngs who were flocking to see his new star. And so Yankee Stadium was built in time for the 1923 season. Built in just 284 days, the House that Ruth Built would one day become associated with some of the greatest achievements in all of sports.

Shea

By the 1960s the Stadium was far from the gold standard in sports facilities. A decline in the quality of the surrounding neighborhood, the local highways, and the public transportation system, coupled with inadequate parking and a crumbling physical structure, had cast a dreary gloom over the once great edifice. State of the Art ballparks from the time of the construction of Yankee Stadium were falling by the wayside to be replaced by facilities better suited for the times. Even the Polo Grounds fell into disuse after the 1963 season. Modern wonders like the new Astrodome in Houston and practical multi-sport stadiums were about to become the norm. The opening of the crisply painted Shea Stadium in 1964 provided a local example of the differences between a fun, modern, and clean ballpark and the stodgy old structure in the Bronx.

Yankee Stadium was given a brief and relatively minor facelift after the 1966 season. A fresh coat of paint was applied, and repairs to the most significant structural issues were completed during the off season. George Steinbrenner wanted something much more suitable for the sport's greatest franchise and he used the threat of relocating the historic franchise across the river to the New Jersey Meadowlands as one of a series of negotiations with the city of New York for either a new stadium or for a major renovation to the existing facility. Negotiations with the city finally produced a positive outcome, and by 1973 a deal was struck with the city of New York to completely refurbish the old structure. The complexities of the task were enormous – a stadium that took 284 days to build from scratch in 1922 would take two years to renovate, leaving the Yankees without a home field for 1974 and 1975. For the plan to work, the Yankees would need a temporary home for those two seasons. Shea Stadium was the logical choice, and an agreement was struck to make the New York

Mets the temporary landlords of the rival Yankees. As tenants in Shea the Yankees would pay their landlord $1 per year, $760 per game, and $61,560 per year for maintenance. The Mets would also retain food and other concession rights, delivering another $600,000 per year in additional revenue, courtesy of the Yankees.

The 1973 season featured a series of events designed to celebrate the fiftieth anniversary of Yankee Stadium. On Opening Day, eighty-three year-old Bob Shawkey, the Yankee starting pitcher for the first game ever played in the Stadium in 1923, and seventy-eight year-old Whitey Witt, the first Yankee ever to bat in the Stadium, were joined by Babe Ruth's widow for the first of a series of events honoring the beloved ballpark. The club's iconic annual Old Timer's Day featured a representative from every Yankee team to play in the stadium, a gathering of many of the greatest living players in the history of baseball. On September 30, the final game of the season was played. The Yankees were woefully unprepared for the chaos that ensued. Souvenir hunters plundered the stadium after the final out, overwhelming the limited security forces and taking everything that wasn't nailed down (and many things that were). When the surreal scene was over the Yankees packed their belongings for the move across town.

Smart teams build their rosters based upon the nuances of their home park, where they play half of their 162 game season. The Yankees had for decades built their club around left handed power, designed to exploit the short Yankee Stadium right field fence, and left-handed pitching, designed to force visiting teams to overload their lineups with right-handed bats aimed at one of the deepest left-center fields in the modern game. Shea Stadium was quite a different beast. It was also built on a swamp, a fact that Yankee outfielders would soon have to deal with. And life in the New York Jets locker room, repurposed as the temporary home of the Yankee home team clubhouse, added to the players' feeling of being a permanent visiting team.

Like it or not and with all of its drawbacks, Shea Stadium was going to be the home of the New York Yankees for the next two seasons.

April

Yankee management was far from satisfied with the twenty-five man roster assembled for opening day of 1974. When the club arrived for the season opener at Shea Stadium on April 6, the stated goal of upgrading several key positions was still only partially met. The left side of the infield seemed to be settled for the time being, with Graig Nettles and Jim Mason opening the season at third base and shortstop. Gene Michael had won the starting second base job in spring training, and veteran Mike Hegan was awarded the first base job by default since there were no other natural first basemen on the roster to offer serious competition. Both players remained in Gabe Paul's crosshairs as the season began, with Horace Clarke and Bill Sudakis standing by as reserves. The group of outfielders collected by Gabe Paul gave manager Virdon lots of options. Bobby Murcer and Roy White started the year as the regulars in center and left field, with Lou Piniella, Ron Blomberg, Elliott Maddox, and Walt Williams backing them up and rotating through right field. Thurman Munson was entrenched as always behind home plate, with Duke Sims and Rick Dempsey available for those rare opportunities when the star catcher took a day off. Jim Ray Hart was among the last cuts of spring training, resulting in a revolving door of designated hitters – eight different men would start games in that role over the course of the season, more than at any other position.

The Yankees were one of only two eastern division teams to carry ten pitchers, with other clubs limiting their staffs to just nine. Mel Stottlemyre, Doc Medich, Pat Dobson, and Steve Kline won spots as the initial starting rotation. Fritz Peterson and Sam McDowell added depth to the rotation, while Ken Wright, Fred Beene, and Tom Buskey rounded out a bullpen headed by Sparky Lyle. Despite the misgivings of Yankee management, it was not a bad roster at all.

With the roster settled for the time being, the Yankees set about their work by opening the season against division rival Cleveland on April 6. The team got out of the gate quickly, winning their first four games and outscoring their opponents 21-5. In the season's first two weeks the team had represented themselves quite well – not overwhelming, but far better than the team that had staggered into the finish of the previous season. Mel Stottlemyre won three of his first four starts and the rest of the pitching staff seemed up to the task ahead.

Of all of the optimistic signs apparent during those first two weeks of the season, none would have as much lasting consequence as the early performance of Lou Piniella. It did not take long for Piniella to emerge as a perfect fit within the Yankee lineup and the clubhouse. Expressing his desire to do "whatever the Yankees wanted," Piniella approached his craft with an intensity second to no one except perhaps teammate Munson. When the club headed north Piniella began the season as a part-timer, but after two weeks in that role his .409 batting average helped force him into the daily lineup. Piniella's style of play and his ability to hit made him an instant darling of previously skeptical Yankee fans, beginning a love affair between New Yorkers and the fiery outfielder that would last beyond Piniella's retirement a decade later. As a side benefit, Piniella's defense, never his strong suit, improved significantly under Bill Virdon's tutelage, and Piniella soon ranked among the league leaders in outfield assists. Quite unexpectedly, Sweet Lou had become an emblem of the new breed of New York Yankee.

April 20, 1974	W	L	PCT	GB
Milwaukee Brewers	7	3	.700	-
Boston Red Sox	7	5	.583	1
New York Yankees	8	6	.571	1
Baltimore Orioles	6	5	.545	1.5
Detroit Tigers	4	8	.333	4
Cleveland Indians	4	9	.308	4.5

The Friday Night Massacre

The traditional role of a first baseman in a major league lineup is to drive the offense. Base running ability, good glove work, and "small ball" skills are nice, but they are no substitute for powerful offensive production. A census of American League first basemen in 1974 would yield names like George Scott, Dick Allen, John Mayberry, Boog Powel, and Carl Yastrzemski – sluggers all. Giving up offense at first base meant playing with a handicap, particularly with a lineup with other offensive weak spots. Gabe Paul understood this as well as anybody, and from the moment he arrived in the Yankee front office he recognized the need to find a suitable occupant for first base. That particular need had largely been unmet since the departure of Joe Pepitone after the 1969 season. Paul worked the phones hard, but could do no better for most of 1973 than a committee consisting of the aging Alou brothers and Ron Blomberg. The latter was more than suitable offensively, but his hopelessly abysmal glove work made him an intolerable long-term option. In desperation Lee MacPhail acquired former Yankee Mike Hegan, a former understudy to Pepitone, late in the 1973 season. Hegan had spent most of his career as a part-timer who had reached double-digits in home runs only once, and that had been five years earlier. Still, Hegan started the last thirty-one games of 1973 at first base and hit a respectable .275. Hegan was not the Yankees preferred choice to open the following season at first, but once again no suitable upgrade could be found. With the opening of the 1974 season, Bill Virdon begrudgingly wrote Hegan's name into the starting lineup for thirteen of the team's first nineteen games. With Hegan hitting a paltry .226 with limited power production, a move of some sort was inevitable.

Yankee Resurrection

Despite Hegan's slow start the Yankees were playing reasonably well by the time the Texas Rangers visited Shea Stadium for a weekend series in late April. As expected, the four man starting rotation of Mel Stottlemyre, Pat Dobson, Doc Medich, and Steve Kline was performing well. Though not overpowering, the quartet helped the club rise above the .500 level and pitched well enough to make almost every game competitive. The sole weakness in the starting rotation was that it was comprised entirely of right handers. Fritz Peterson, the lefty who had helped anchor the rotation for the last eight years, was noticeably absent from the rotation when the season began. Fritz Peterson was one of the more underrated players of his day. A victim of poor timing, Peterson arrived in New York in 1966 just as the Yankee decline was in full swing. He joined the starting rotation in his rookie season and averaged thirty-three starts and fourteen wins a year from 1966-1973. During his peak seasons of 1969-1972 he averaged seventeen wins, delivered a twenty win season, twice posted the best Walks and Hits per Innings Pitched (WHIP) ratio in the American League, and had made an All-Star team. Still, he largely flew under the radar and had missed out on being recognized for his rightful spot among the game's top left-handed starting pitchers. Unfortunately for all involved, Peterson's strong personality did not endear him to the new management team. In each of the first two seasons under the Steinbrenner regime Peterson engaged in bitter contract disputes, the kind in which neither side walks out feeling like a winner. Peterson's contract battles further tarnished his already damaged reputation in the eyes of a new Yankee management team that had never fully forgiven him for the family swap scandal from the year before. Peterson, for his part, also sensed that his association with the club was in jeopardy. By the spring of 1974 his salary issues, his headline-grabbing domestic situation, a seventeen loss 1973 season, and his standing as one of the popular members of the clubhouse "country club" had placed him squarely on the trading block. In the first month of the season he appeared in only three games, starting only one of them. Peterson not only read the writing on the wall, he embraced it. Seeing Gabe Paul discussing potential personnel swaps with Chicago White Sox general manager Roland Hemond, Peterson called out to Hemond and said "Please take me!!!" Peterson directly asked Gabe Paul to trade him – specifically, to trade him anywhere but Cleveland.

"Cleveland? Oh, no. We would *never* do that to you." the Smiling Cobra reportedly responded.

On the evening of Friday, April 26, the Yankees were celebrating a 4-3 victory over the Texas Rangers. Management had kept the players uneasy with their constant public disclosures that they were looking to make deals, but nobody expected the bombshell that would explode that evening. It started when Pete Sheehy told Peterson and fellow pitchers Steve Kline, Tom Buskey, and Fred Beene to report to the manager's office. The four pitchers were baffled, unsure of what infraction could have caused their being summoned by Virdon after a victory. They were shocked when they hear the news – the four of them had been packaged in a trade with Cleveland for first baseman Chris Chambliss and right-handed pitchers Dick Tidrow and Cecil Upshaw. Their teammates were equally stunned, though not speechless. One by one they clearly expressed their dissatisfaction with the deal. Bobby Murcer: "I can't believe this trade." Thurman Munson: "They've got to be kidding." Even Mel Stottlemyre, a total stranger to controversy and among the least outspoken players in baseball: "You just don't trade four pitchers. You just don't."

But they did.

The trade was incredibly logical from a Yankee perspective. Peterson was a non-entity with the club. Steve Kline had demonstrated enough potential for the Yankees to part with Stan Bahnsen three years earlier, and Kline rewarded their faith by posting a 16-9 mark in 1972. But an arm injury had set him back, and the Yankees feared he was damaged goods and that his value was declining rapidly. Rookie Tom Buskey had posted decent numbers as he progressed through the minor leagues but had never shown enough upward potential to garner much excitement from the Yankee brass. Freddie Beene was perhaps the most valuable member of the group departing to Cleveland. A utility pitcher, the popular and diminutive Beene could start, pitch long relief, and close out games, sometimes all in the same week. In one game on a blistering hot afternoon in 1973, Beene relieved starter Fritz Peterson after Fritz injured himself fielding a bunt single on the first batter of the game. Beene went on to pitch nine complete innings in relief for the win. Appreciative of the fact that as a five-foot nine-inch pitcher he was lucky to be in the major leagues at all, Beene was content to fill any role the Yankees threw at him. On the whole, the Yankees were giving up four pitchers whose aggregate potential contribution was relatively limited.

Chris Chambliss was the key to the trade. Chambliss was highly coveted by Paul, who was familiar with his work in Cleveland. Paul saw the twenty-five year-old Chambliss as a potential batting champion who could be a fixture at first base for years to come. The lefty hitter had broken into the major leagues in 1971 by succeeding new teammate Thurman Munson as the Rookie of the Year. He had provided solid offense and excellent defense at first base over the next two seasons, but he had not yet experienced a true breakout season. He was hitting .328 at the time of the trade, but had no home runs to his credit and was generally not known as a power hitter. Cleveland hated to lose him, but badly needed bodies for their pitching staff. In addition, they had concluded that former Yankee John Ellis, acquired in the Graig Nettles trade a year earlier and now serving as one of Chambliss's backups, was more than ready to assume the everyday role, an irony that could not have been lost on Gabe Paul. Tidrow had been named the top rookie pitcher in the American League in 1972, winning a total of twenty-eight games over his first two seasons and starting a remarkable forty games in 1972. Tidrow would easily slide into Kline's spot in the starting rotation and his durability was a welcomed relief from Kline's shaky health. Veteran reliever Upshaw would replace the tandem of Beene and Buskey, providing a veteran presence with postseason experience in the bullpen. The Yankees counted on the contribution of Upshaw and Tidrow and the good health of the remaining pitchers to offset the loss of the four hurlers.

In addition to the logic of the move there was a not-so-subtle subtext to this trade. The four pitchers, particularly the veteran Peterson, were popular with their teammates. They were all members in good standing in the "country club," and their removal from the picture was a reinforcement of a prevailing theme – things were going to change in Yankeeland and the survivors had better get with the new program or they would be the next to go. It was a message that was clearly received, though it was not a message that was welcomed. The resentment level within the

Yankee clubhouse increased, making life difficult for the newcomers. Gabe Paul was unmoved, even as Yankee fans joined in the chorus of voices criticizing the deal. Chambliss ended up catching the brunt of the ire from the stands. Often booed that first season, Chambliss struggled at the plate but never crumbled under the pressure as a lesser man might have done.

New faces had arrived, old friends had left, and a proverbial bucket of cold water had been dumped on the heads of the players caught in between.

And it was still only April.

April 26, 1974	W	L	PCT	GB
Baltimore Orioles	10	6	.625	-
New York Yankees	11	8	.579	0.5
Milwaukee Brewers	8	6	.571	1
Boston Red Sox	9	9	.500	2
Detroit Tigers	6	10	.375	4
Cleveland Indians	6	11	.353	4.5

The Tugboat

Diana Munson has a clear, insightful explanation for the lasting love affair between Yankee fans and her late husband. "Thurman was a throwback. He was confident, cocky, and gave everything he had. New York fans are smart and you can't fool them. They can spot someone who isn't authentic and see through them in a second." He was also a great ballplayer, an answer to a desperate prayer from Yankee fans for someone to help lead them back to their glory days.

Throughout their dynasty years the Yankees were graced with three of the greatest catchers in the history of the game – Bill Dickey, Yogi Berra, and Elston Howard. The fact that the careers of Berra and Howard overlapped for almost a decade was also a tribute to the depth of the organization. All three of these remarkable men also possessed a remarkable presence in the clubhouse – all three would become Yankee coaches and Dickey and Berra also managed the team. Howard may well have one day followed them into the managerial ranks had his life not been cut short at the age of fifty-one. In fact, such was the power of Howard's presence that he earned points in the Most Valuable Player voting in 1967 despite a .178 batting average, a recognition of his contribution to the late season pennant run by the Boston Red Sox.

Perhaps no other position symbolized the Yankees' fall from the top of the mountain than the decline of the catcher's spot. Howard had earned the American League Most Valuable Player Award in 1963 and followed that with a third place finish in the voting for 1964. But by 1965 he was thirty-six and hurting, another victim of Johnny Keane's panic-stricken habit of running injured stars onto the field rather than letting them heal. The bottom dropped out quickly for Howard, and by August of 1967 he was hitting an anemic .197 with a mere three home runs and seventeen RBI when he was sent to the Boston Red Sox. As a sign of their regard of Howard's value to the franchise, the Yankees predicated the transaction on Boston's promise that when Howard retired from the Red Sox as an active player the Yankees would have the first opportunity to hire him into a non-playing role within their organization.

The Yankees saw the writing on the wall with the aging Berra and Howard in the early 1960s, but inexplicably refrained from stocking their minor league system with a quality replacement. Instead, they decided to convert a twenty-four year-old infielder playing with their AAA Richmond farm club into their catcher of the future.

Jerry Dean "Jake" Gibbs was an All-American quarterback for the University of Mississippi football team. He was named the Southeastern Conference football player of the year and drafted by teams in both the National and American Football Leagues. In addition to playing for a national collegiate champion in football, Gibbs was a key contributor to an SEC championship in baseball. It was this latter credential that brought him to the attention of the New York Yankees, who signed Gibbs in 1961 with one of the largest bonuses in Yankee history. Young Jake Gibbs was on a fast track to the major leagues, having held his own at the AAA level for his first two professional seasons. But the Yankees had other plans. With great respect for Gibbs's athleticism and sudden concern for the lack of a catching pipeline, Gibbs was moved from the left side of the infield to a spot behind home plate for the 1963 season. This crash course in learning what is arguably the most challenging position on the field stymied Gibbs's development as a hitter and caused his career to stall, resulting in him spending parts of five straight seasons at the AAA level. After cups of coffee as a September call up in 1962, 1963, and 1964, Gibbs was promoted to the big club to stay in mid-1965. There he was able to hone his catching skills under the guidance of Elston Howard and Yankee coach Jim Hegan while he warmed the bench. By then Gibbs seemed destined to disappoint the Yankees by failing to reach the potential befitting his $100,000 signing bonus. Worse, his crash course in catching was resulting in multiple injuries, including a broken finger that robbed him of a chance to suit up for the 1964 World Series and a broken arm resulting from a backswing by a hitter in 1966 (the home plate umpire during the latter incident observed that "Gibbs was too close" to the hitter). Ready or not, Jake Gibbs became the team's number one catcher in 1967, sharing the role first with Howard and later with Bob Tillman and Frank Fernandez. Thus, the Yankees had gone from the holy trinity of Dickey, Berra, and Howard to Gibbs, Tillman, and Fernandez. It was a long way to fall.

Despite the decline at the catching position, the Yankees seemed remarkably uninterested or unable to restock the organization's pool of catching talent. In the 1965 free agent draft they drafted five catchers out of their forty picks, none of whom would go on to play a single inning in the majors. They opted to use their first pick to select pitcher Bill Burbach, passing over a promising young catcher named Johnny Bench. Over the next two drafts they drafted a total of seventeen catchers whose collective major league experience would end up being two games. Future catching star Ted Simmons was bypassed by the team in the 1967 draft, as were

Steve Yeager and future Yankee Rick Dempsey. In 1968 they got it right, using their first pick and the fourth overall pick of the draft to select Kent State University star Thurman Munson.

At first glance Thurman Munson might not have looked like a professional athlete, let alone a future star baseball player. Munson was described by his contemporaries in various, uncomplimentary ways – squat, stocky, bow-legged, scruffy, and a host of other terms that paint a picture of an ungraceful figure. Legendary Yankee clubhouse manager Pete Sheehy complained "His rear end is too big for the uniform pants." He had a temperament to match – few, if any, descriptions of Munson's personality omit the word "gruff." Yet behind this frame and this façade was a remarkable athlete whose personality won the hearts of teammates and fans like few others. No less a hard character than Gabe Paul offered this insider's assessment of Munson: "Thurman Munson is a nice guy who doesn't want anyone to know it."

Munson's minor league apprenticeship would be short. He touched up AA Eastern League pitching for a .301 average during his short stay there in 1968. He appeared major league-ready by the spring of 1969, but Uncle Sam called and Munson was dispatched to Army reserve duty for most of the first half of the season. While fulfilling his military obligations, Munson was able to grab some occasional playing time at the AAA level, where he hit a robust .363. The Yankees were absolutely convinced they had found a catcher whose name would fit in with the greats of the organization's storied history.

While the Yankee brass awaited Munson's arrival, his path was cleared by another bright new hope in a catcher's mask. Johnny Ellis was not even drafted by a major league team – he was signed by the Yankees as a roster-filler, someone to plug holes in the rosters of the deep minor leagues. A glaring lack of competition, military duty for Fernandez, Munson, and AAA catcher Lou Howell, and another finger injury for Gibbs cleared the path for Ellis to leap from the Class A Kinston Eagles all the way to the Yankees in May of 1969. The heretofore unknown Ellis immediately captured the hearts and imagination of Yankee fans by hitting an inside-the-park home run in front of the hometown crowd in his very first game. Ellis proved himself capable of playing at the big league level, hitting .300 during his initial stint as Yankee starting catcher. The return of Fernandez and Gibbs resulted in a trip to AAA for Ellis, but Yankee fans now had a cause for optimism in the future of the catcher position.

Ellis's debut in pinstripes was followed by the arrival of Munson in August. By September Munson was the everyday catcher as the Yankees assessed his readiness for major league play. Munson did not disappoint. Despite having only ninety-nine games of professional experience under his belt, Thurman Munson firmly established his hold on the catcher's position. Ellis provided competition for the staring spot in the spring of 1970, winning the Dawson Award as the best rookie in the Yankee camp, but Yankee brass were firmly committed to Munson and it was Munson who held the starting job on Opening Day. Ellis was moved to first base, Gibbs to the bench, and Fernandez to Oakland. The Yankee catcher's box would be the realm of Thurman Munson until the day he died.

Munson's tenure as the anointed star did not begin well. He started his first full season with the team with an unbelievably low .033 mark before he had his first multi-hit game, and he didn't climb above .250 until a four hit game in late May. But Munson rewarded the patience and confidence of the Yankees with a .302 final batting average and a Rookie of the Year trophy.

The affection of Yankee fans for the brash new star was eclipsed only by the affection of his fellow players. From the start he was a force within the Yankee clubhouse. Munson earned the nickname Tugboat, a tribute to both his workhorse attitude and his physical appearance. His work ethic carried him through many hard times and injuries as the years progressed. Bitten by the sophomore jinx in 1971, Munson saw his average plummet by fifty points. He bounced back a year later, and by 1973 had brought his average above the .300 mark and had earned his first of three consecutive gold gloves. He also brought the kind of intensity and winning attitude that would insulate him from criticism from the new owner and general manager – Thurman Munson was a warrior and a winner and the kind of player that the new regime could build around. Though popular, Thurman Munson was not viewed as part of the "country club" that Gabe Paul and George Steinbrenner were committed to destroying.

Munson's work ethic carried a price. The man would not rest. He played tired, and he played hurt. It did not help at all that the Yankees had no suitable backup for him. Gibbs retired after the 1971 season, and John Ellis was part of the package of spare parts sent to Cleveland for Graig Nettles after the 1972 season. Munson started 142 games in 1973, often going a month at a time without a break. The prospects for relief looked no better in 1974. Late in the 1973 season the Yankees acquired veteran Duke Sims as a backup to the fatigued Munson. Never known for his defensive abilities, Sims's lone claim to fame in his brief stay with the Yankees was the fact that he hit the last home run in Yankee Stadium before the ballpark was closed for renovation. Competing with Sims for the role of Munson's backup in the spring of 1974 was twenty-four year-old Rick Dempsey. Dempsey had debuted five years earlier at the age of twenty when he joined the Minnesota Twins as a late season call up. That 1969 appearance set the stage for Dempsey to one day join the short list of players who would appear in games in four different decades. That extended future was far from certain when Dempsey arrived for spring training, as his total major league experience over the past five partial seasons with the Twins and the Yankees was just forty-seven games. In contrast to the good-hit, bad-glove Sims, Dempsey was viewed as a light-hitting defensive specialist. The club decided to carry three catchers as they broke camp in the spring of 1974, with the expectation that the backup catching situation would resolve itself during the regular season. When Dempsey swung a hot bat in his first few appearances of the season and Sims posted a .133 batting average, the backup job went to Dempsey and Sims was shipped to Texas on May 7 in exchange for minor league pitcher Larry Gura and cash. Little did anyone realize at the time, but that trade would one day have enormous consequences for the Yankees.

Even with a more capable backup Munson was still an unmovable fixture in the Yankee lineup. In the final days of spring training he was struck on his throwing hand by a backswing. Munson played through the resulting pain for the entire season, but it clearly impacted his performance. When April drew to a close, Munson's batting average stood at .209 and he had driven in only six runs. Worse still, the injury had played havoc with his ability to throw out runners. The reigning gold glove winner, the player who had gone the entire 1971 season with only a single error, committed twenty-two errors in 1974. Munson, who specialized in picking off sleeping baserunners, threw away four balls in April alone. Still, it was Munson who was the heart and soul of the Yankee lineup and despite his struggles his contribution to the Yankee cause was undeniable. Nothing was going to keep Thurman Munson on the sidelines.

While Munson struggled in the early days of the season, Graig Nettles sizzled. After hitting seventy-one home runs in three seasons with Cleveland, Nettles failed to pepper the short porch in Yankee Stadium to the level expected when he was acquired. Though he had hit a respectable twenty-two home runs, Nettles struggled through much of his first season as a Yankee with his average dipping below .200 as late as June. Despite a stronger second half in 1973, Graig Nettles had something to prove to Yankee fans and Yankee management when the 1974 season began. In contrast to his slow 1973 start, Nettles was red hot out of the gate in 1974. Nettles opened the year by hitting a robust .301 during the month of April, up almost one hundred points from the first month of the prior season. Home runs also seemed to come easier for Nettles as he hit four home runs in a double header on April 14 and home runs in three consecutive games from April 19-21. By the time the month was over Nettles was leading the league with eleven home runs, a record at that time for the month of April. Comparisons began to appear in the local press between Nettles' home run pace and the pace of Yankee legends Roger Maris and Babe Ruth during their record home run seasons. Such talk was premature at best, as Nettles returned to earth and went homerless in the month of May. Still, the lefty slugger's bat carried the team through the first month of the season and showed that he was indeed a long term answer to the Yankees third base problem.

April 30, 1974	W	L	PCT	GB
Baltimore Orioles	11	8	.579	-
New York Yankees	13	10	.565	-
Milwaukee Brewers	9	8	.529	1
Cleveland Indians	10	11	.476	2
Detroit Tigers	9	10	.474	2
Boston Red Sox	10	12	.455	2.5

Power Shortage

The very mention of Yankee Stadium conjures up images of the left-handed power hitters so prominently featured in the Yankee lineup throughout the club's history. The stadium was, after all, The House That Ruth Built, and when the Yankees played their last game before the renovation of Yankee Stadium the lefty hitting Ruth was still the all-time major league home run leader. With its short right field porch, the park was considered heaven on earth for lefties inclined to pull the ball down the line. The reality was that famous Yankee lefties (or switch hitters) like Ruth, Gehrig, Berra, Mantle, Maris, Pepitone, Tresh, and Murcer could hit the ball out of any ballpark that they played in. Nevertheless, the baseball world saw the short Yankee Stadium right field porch as a distinct advantage for a team that played half of its games in that park and the Yankees would routinely stuff their roster with lefty pull hitters who could leverage that advantage and pad the home team line on the scoreboard. While the Athletics were still in Kansas City, owner Charlie Finley even went so far as to try to pull his team's right field fence in to match the dimensions of Yankee Stadium. When he was ordered by the American League to push the fences back to the required minimum dimensions (Yankee Stadium and other older ballparks were grandfathered and were not subject to the newer rules), Finley reluctantly complied, but also ordered that a white line be drawn where the shortened fence had been located and ordered his public address announcer to inform the crowd that any ball caught or landing between that line and the fence would have been a home run in Yankee Stadium.

Power Shortage

Despite the gamesmanship of Finley and the opinion of the pundits, the reality of the impact of the short right field fence on Yankee fortunes was much different. To begin with, the Yankees were no longer a team whose success rested primarily on home runs. With the exception of two seasons at the height of the roster depletions of World War II, the Yankees had hit more than one hundred home runs in each season from 1925-1968. That streak ended in 1969, and the team again fell below the one hundred home run mark in 1971. Their ninety-four home runs in 1969 was the lowest total (again with the exception of World War II) since Babe Ruth had joined the club in 1920. In the last twenty years that the Yankees played in the original Yankee Stadium, they hit more home runs on the road than at home a staggering thirteen times. During their last five-year stretch of winning American League pennants from 1960-1964, the Yankees hit more homers on the road than at home every single year, with a differential of twenty-four home runs in 1964. The home club's production of home runs at Yankee Stadium bottomed out in 1971 and in the strike-shortened 1972 season, when they hit just thirty-nine and thirty-three home runs in their home ballpark. In both seasons the team had greater long ball production on the road. The trend reversed in 1973, when the team had their best total home run year since 1966 and the second highest percentage of Yankee Stadium home runs in two decades. Still, the history and related statistics indicated that the move to the more spacious Shea Stadium should have minimal impact on Yankee power.

While ruminating on the impact of the move to Shea on Yankee hitters, the pundits conveniently overlooked the potential impact on Yankee pitching. As Yankee home run production declined, the club became more and more dependent upon good pitching to keep the team competitive. As Yankee power bottomed out, Mel Stottlemyre, Fritz Peterson, Stan Bahnsen, and Steve Kline formed the nucleus of an effective starting rotation ably supported by the likes of Jack Aker, Lindy McDaniel, and Sparky Lyle in the bullpen. Together they had kept the Yankees competitive at a time when clubs with similarly anemic production were falling to the bottom of the standings. In their final season in the original Yankee Stadium, Yankee pitchers gave up twenty-five more runs on the road than at home and had a collective Earned Run Average of more than one run per game higher in games played outside of the Bronx. If anyone should have been concerned about the impact of missing the old ballpark, it should have been the pitching staff.

Despite predictions that the Yankee left handed bats would be neutralized by the move away from the friendly Yankee Stadium right field porch, the Yankees adjusted to their temporary home by hitting a club record twenty-seven home runs in April, surpassing the previous high for April of twenty-four set way back in 1932. The historic power surge by Graig Nettles provided the bedrock for this power performance, with the remaining home runs spread throughout the lineup. With the change of the calendar to May, however, home run production plummeted. The entire club managed only nine round-trippers in May, one of the lowest monthly totals for the club since the dead ball era. Shea Stadium's generous dimensions could not be blamed for this remarkable change of fortune — of the nine home runs, seven came at home and only two, including one by the light-hitting Jim Mason, came on the road.

While Yankee hitters struggled with inconsistency, the Yankee front office struggled with trying to find the right pieces to complete the Yankee roster puzzle. With players still reeling from the Friday Night Massacre, Gabe Paul remained hard at work trying to fill remaining gaps with very few established players available on the market. Paul had reinforced his Dial-a-Deal image in the eyes of Yankee players, and Manager Bill Virdon compared Paul to Frank "Trader" Lane, a general manager who was known for an insatiable appetite for trading and who had traded Virdon from the St. Louis Cardinals to the Pittsburgh Pirates twenty years earlier.

Nervous and unhappy players craved stability. An impatient front office craved victory and change. Front offices win these confrontations, and in light of that fact and the fact that the Yankees continued to be stuck in neutral in the divisional standings, it was a sure bet that more change was on the way.

May 15, 1974	W	L	PCT	GB
Milwaukee Brewers	15	14	.517	-
Baltimore Orioles	16	15	.516	-
Detroit Tigers	16	15	.516	-
Cleveland Indians	17	16	.515	-
New York Yankees	18	19	.486	1.0
Boston Red Sox	16	18	.471	1.5

The Face of the Franchise

Though baseball salaries were on the rise by the time George Steinbrenner purchased the Yankees, an annual salary of $100,000 still marked a dividing line that separated the games very best in the game from the rest of the pack. Only twenty-eight men, comprising less than five percent of the major league rosters, had reached or exceeded that salary level for the 1973 season. Of those who had, more than two-thirds would reach the Hall of Fame, and that does not include controversial Hall exclusions Dick Allen and Pete Rose. Among those on the $100K list who did not achieve enshrinement in Cooperstown was homegrown Yankee star Bobby Murcer. Murcer's presence as a member of such an esteemed group was in part the product of the enormous popularity of Murcer in the eyes of Yankee fans and Murcer's standing as the heir to Mickey Mantle. The combination of his pedigree, star-level performance, and a genuine love affair between the hardened New York fans and the likeable country boy from Oklahoma made him the centerpiece of the Yankee roster. An impartial observer focused purely on statistical performance could easily conclude that of everyone on the $100,000 salary list, Murcer's performance on the field did not warrant such a distinction. In any event, Bobby Murcer was the face of the New York Yankee franchise. In the years immediately after Mickey Mantle's retirement, Murcer was one of the few reasons for fans to stay loyal to the club and make the effort to come out to the ballpark. Unfortunately, George Steinbrenner and Gabe Paul, though appreciative of drawing cards, were the kind of executives who demanded performance commensurate with compensation and in their eyes Bobby Murcer was taking home an elite paycheck without delivering elite production. In addition, their desire to recreate *their*

Yankee team in *their* image did not jive with Murcer as the face of *their* franchise. A brief holdout prior to the start of the 1974 season made matters worse. Murcer walked away the winner of a $20,000 raise, making him the highest paid Yankee in history. George Steinbrenner made no secret that he expected Murcer to earn that salary, both on the field and as a more disciplined leader in the clubhouse. The addition of newly arrived Manager Bill Virdon to the mix did not help – Ralph Houk had managed and mentored Murcer for most of Murcer's time at the big league level and the Yankee star was very comfortable playing under Houk. Virdon was in many ways Houk's polar opposite, and a collision course between the star outfielder and the new manager had been charted.

Bobby Murcer's rise to prominence had been predicted from the moment he was signed in 1964. Just barely eighteen years old, Murcer was one of the last Yankee signings prior to the introduction of the amateur draft a year later. The Murcer package came with its own built-in legend. Murcer hailed from the same area of Oklahoma as legendary Yankee predecessor Mickey Mantle. A further parallel was forged by the fact that he was signed by the same scout who had signed Mantle (ironically, that same scout, Tom Greenwade, also signed Bill Virdon to a Yankee contract). Like Mantle, Murcer was also signed as a shortstop. As is so often the case, such circumstances bring great expectations, which in turn bring great pressures. These pressures, and an unwelcomed skeleton in Mantle's closet, delayed and almost completely derailed Murcer's date with Yankee destiny.

Faced with the decline and premature retirement of star shortstop Tony Kubek, Murcer's apprenticeship in the minor leagues was cut short.

Yankee Resurrection

He annihilated Carolina League pitching in his one full season in the minors in 1965, and there were signs that he could handle major league pitching during a brief September call up. There were also glaring signs that his glove was anything but major league-ready as he committed five errors in just eleven games, which extrapolates to almost seventy-five errors in a full season. In response to the retirement of Kubek after that season, the Yankees acquired veteran Ruben Amaro to keep the shortstop position warm while Murcer mastered the defensive skills necessary for the position, with the expectation that Murcer would become the full time shortstop a year later in 1967. That plan fell apart in the fifth game of the 1966 season when Amaro suffered a devastating knee injury, thrusting the ill-prepared Murcer into the limelight and into the starting shortstop job. It was a disaster. Proving that his defensive performance during his previous audition was no fluke, Murcer committed three errors in his debut start after the Amaro injury, errors that cost the Yankees the game. Displaying a lack of patience that would have made future owner George Steinbrenner proud, manager Johnny Keane benched Murcer and he was eventually sent down to AAA Toledo to work on his defense. Murcer returned to the Yankees in September, starting fourteen games at shortstop with the expectation that the full-time shortstop job would be his the following spring. It was then that a largely forgotten incident from Mickey Mantle's Oklahoma past would rise to bite him.

One of the commonalities between Murcer and Mantle was the fact that they entered the major leagues during a time of war. In Mantle's case the Korean War was in full fury and America's young men were being drafted in large numbers. Mantle, to the amazement of many, was characterized as medically unfit, originally due to chronic osteomyelitis and later due to the serious knee injury that he suffered in the 1951 World Series. Mantle's detractors could not comprehend how one of the finest young athletes in America could somehow be medically unfit for military service and accused the youngster of being a draft-dodger. The unwanted attention embarrassed Mantle, and it also embarrassed the officials on the Oklahoma draft board.

Fast forward fifteen years to 1967 when new Yankee Bobby Murcer was facing a low draft number and a rapidly escalating war in Viet Nam. The Yankees, unwilling to lose a budding star who was such an important figure in the planned rebuilding of their franchise, arranged for a place in an Army reserve unit for Murcer, a practice employed by many major league teams at that time. With memories of the Mickey Mantle story still burning their conscience, the draft board in Oklahoma made sure that the processing of Murcer's orders to report for regular Army duty were handled expeditiously, and it was into the regular Army Murcer was inducted. The difference was significant – reservists would miss occasional blocks of time, but were generally able to balance reserve duty with their "day job" as a ballplayer. For Murcer, being drafted by the regular Army meant two full years away from the game. There was nothing that Murcer, or the Yankees, could do – despite Yankee attempts to intercede, Bobby Murcer's baseball career would be put on hold for at least two years. From a baseball perspective, this course of events was devastating to Murcer and the Yankees. There would be no guarantee that Murcer would return to form after a two year hiatus, and Murcer's predecessor Tony Kubek had suffered his career-ending injury while on military reserve duty (albeit in a game of touch football, not military combat).

Yankee Resurrection

As it turned out, Murcer's detour from the road to the majors may have been a blessing in disguise. During his two years of Army service, Murcer matured emotionally and grew physically. The immense pressure that would have been on him, literally playing across the field from Mantle, may have crushed the young player. Now that pressure was replaced by joyful anticipation over his return in the spring of 1969, and Murcer was much more prepared physically and mentally to assume the role planned for him. The Yankees recognized that perhaps the shortstop role was not a good match for Murcer, particularly given his strong but dangerously wild throwing arm. The club instead decided to put him at third base where there was much less pressure and much less risk. It was at third base that Murcer opened the 1969 season, and from the start he was atop the league leader board in most offensive categories, far exceeding even the most optimistic expectations for his bat. Unfortunately, his glove and throwing arm exceeded even the worst fears of the club. Fourteen errors in his first thirty-one games at third base equaled the horrific pace from his initial call up four years earlier. Desperate to keep his bat in the lineup while minimizing the damage he was doing with his defense, manager Ralph Houk decided to move Murcer to right field, a position in which he had no professional experience. The gamble paid off – Murcer quickly adapted to the position without letting the move to a new position interfere with his progress as a hitter. In fact, Murcer took so well to his new role that Houk began to test Murcer in center field as the season wound down. Murcer continued to impress with his adaptation to the outfield, and by the end of the season he was the everyday center fielder, truly following in the footsteps of Mickey Mantle.

The Face of the Franchise

Murcer continued to deliver very solid offensive production as he anchored the Yankee lineup. He narrowly missed winning an American League batting title in 1971, following that performance with a second place finish in the home run race a year later. As a sign of his competence as a center fielder, Murcer was awarded a Gold Glove Award in 1972. Murcer was clearly a fan favorite, and he basked in the attention. Murcer parlayed his on the field performance and his dynamic personality to become recognized as the soul of the Yankees both on the field and in the clubhouse. Still, Gabe Paul and George Steinbrenner were not impressed and saw Murcer as part of the problem, a symbol of the Good Old Boys atmosphere that had the Yankees stuck in a decade-long rut. If Murcer was indeed the soul of the clubhouse, George Steinbrenner expected more aggressive leadership from his highest paid and highest profile player. Steinbrenner was still a few years away from his controversial decision to force Thurman Munson into the role of Captain of the Yankees, but he was already laying the framework for designating a first among equals by making it clear to Murcer that he expected his highest paid star to be a Steinbrenner-like leader in the clubhouse. Even Murcer acknowledged that he might be expected to "kick a few butts," but the affable Murcer was not the butt-kicking type. The trademark rocking chair that sat in front of Murcer's locker perfectly symbolized his laid back demeanor, and to Bobby's Yankee teammates he would always be the likeable, fun, good old boy from Oklahoma.

Despite the expectations of Yankee players and Yankee fans, neither Steinbrenner, Paul, nor new manager Bill Virdon were going to be bound by Bobby Murcer's pre-ordained destiny to carry a torch handed over from an earlier time. If Bobby Murcer had to be knocked down a couple of rungs for the Yankees to break through to the top of the standings, the new leadership team would not hesitate to do it.

As Murcer soaked in the adoration of the Yankee fan base and did his best to ignore the slight shadow cast by the new leadership team, he had a more practical issue to deal with. Almost from the moment of the announcement that the Yankees would spend two seasons as temporary occupants of Shea Stadium, one question loomed large among the huge pool of beat reporters covering the club: "How will Bobby Murcer's home run production fare away from the lefty-friendly right field fence of Yankee Stadium?" This was not a far-fetched question – nineteen of his twenty-two home runs had come at home the previous season, a number that might be driven less by the short right field porch than by the fact that Murcer loved hitting in his home park, as evidenced by the fact that his overall batting average was fifty-five points higher at home than on the road and he recorded almost three quarters of his RBI in his home park. Still, the thought weighed heavy on his mind from the beginning of spring training. He admitted to the press that he would miss hitting in his favorite ballpark, though he insisted he was not worried about hitting in Shea Stadium. Those closest to him suggested that he might be whistling through a graveyard and that he was hiding his own concern that he would be playing half a season in a park that was forty-five feet deeper at the right field foul pole and twenty-seven feet deeper in the right field power alley than the field in which he had been so successful. A batting practice session in Shea Stadium shortly before the season opener did nothing but hurt his confidence, as balls that would have easily cleared the right field fence in the Bronx fell short of the warning track in Queens. The situation went from bad to worse once the season began. Murcer made solid, consistent contact throughout the first month of the season, falling slightly below the .300 mark as April wound down. Despite this solid batting average, Murcer's worst fears about a decline in home run output came to fruition. In the first month of the season he managed only two home runs, both of which came in a double header in Cleveland. His only other extra base hit during the first month of the season was a triple at Shea on April 28. Things went from terrible to worse than terrible in May, when he went homerless both at home and on the road. His batting average fell fifty points, and with every day that passed the speculation that Shea Stadium had played havoc with the star's confidence seemed to carry more and more weight. While Murcer struggled offensively, Yankee management was about to make matters even worse for their star outfielder.

Nothing in Elliott Maddox's background had prepared the Yankees and their fans for the breakthrough season he was to experience in 1974. Noted primarily for his defense, Maddox had cracked the .250 mark only once in four seasons with the Tigers, Senators, and Rangers. The arrival of Billy Martin in Texas ended any hope that Maddox had of holding a starting role with the Rangers. The relationship between Martin and Maddox got off to a bad start and deteriorated from there, resolved only with the sale of Maddox to the Yankees in the spring of 1974.

The ink on the press release announcing the acquisition of Maddox wasn't even dry when speculation over whether the Yankees would recognize his stature as the top defensive outfielder on the club and use him in a manner consistent with that fact. For the moment the club seemed to be deep with outfielders. Roy White and Murcer played virtually every day, and Ron Blomberg and Lou Piniella shared most of the workload in right field through mid-May. Maddox and Walt Williams warmed the bench, with Maddox making an occasional start in between appearances as a pinch hitter, pinch runner, and late inning defensive replacement in right field. By May 22 Maddox had not started a game in almost a month and was hitting just .222 when Virdon put him into the lineup in right field, moving Piniella to left in place of the slumping White. Maddox made the most of the opportunity, going 3-4 with a walk. The next night he was back in the lineup, this time in the leadoff spot. Nobody realized it at the time, but Maddox was about to change the whole face of the Yankee offense and defense. On the twenty-sixth of May Virdon "rested" Murcer in the first game of a double-header against Baltimore, moving Maddox to center field. Although Murcer returned to his spot in center field for the nightcap, he found himself on the bench again the next day as Maddox once again assumed the starting role in center. Murcer thought nothing of it until the next day, when he read the posted lineup in the clubhouse and saw "Maddox – Center Field, Murcer – Right Field." Murcer was livid at not having been consulted, or at least verbally informed, about the loss of his beloved role in center field. In stark contrast to Virdon's lack of communication with Murcer, Ralph Houk had taken Murcer aside and carefully explained the club's rationale in moving him to the outfield five years earlier. Hearing about that change from the manager directly certainly softened the blow, but once again Virdon's personality and approach to communicating with players was completely different to Houk's player-focused style. Murcer confronted Virdon, and the manager's explanation to him was simple – "It is the best thing for the club" and "That's the way I want it." Virdon made it clear that it was not a decision that was up for debate, and he also made it clear that Murcer's benching in two of the last three games was no coincidence – if Murcer didn't like his new role he could continue to taste life from the bench. Murcer was far less than thrilled with the new arrangement, but had no choice but to suck it up, put on as happy a face as possible, and do everything necessary to win. Still, Murcer was human and the move irreparably damaged his relationship with Virdon as well as with Elliott Maddox, to a point where Maddox later claimed that Murcer never spoke socially with him again. Many Yankee players sided with Murcer, and Virdon's reputation in the eyes of Yankee players as a hard ass was even stronger than before. The manager was unmoved – he was brought in to win, and in his eyes a strong outfield defense was an essential part of a winning team and this was the best defensive lineup. Yankee players would soon be forced to agree.

Once again the world of diehard Yankee fans was shaken, more so than even the stunning Friday Night Massacre. It was a given that Bobby Murcer would be the Yankee starting center fielder for the remainder of what was expected to be a long and glorious career, ending with a plaque in the outfield alongside those of predecessors Mickey Mantle and Joe DiMaggio. And if the end of the dream was to come prematurely, surely it would not end at the hands of a guy from New Jersey named Elliott Maddox. If baseball lineups were popularity contests, Bobby Murcer's job would be safe forever. But once again the new

Yankee regime chose to do the controversial, unpopular thing that was more likely to win ballgames. And while it might have been initially hard for Yankee fans and Yankee players to accept the change, the Yankees were a markedly better club with Elliott Maddox at the top of the lineup and patrolling center field. The reality was that the Yankee outfield had become one of the best in the league, literally overnight.

May 28, 1974	W	L	PCT	GB
Boston Red Sox	25	20	.556	-
Milwaukee Brewers	23	19	.548	0.5
Detroit Tigers	22	22	.500	2.5
Cleveland Indians	22	23	.489	3
Baltimore Orioles	21	23	.477	3.5
New York Yankees	23	26	.469	4

The Scapegoat

It is sometimes convenient to overlook the fact that even the very worst major league baseball player is infinitely better than the vast majority of men who set out to become professional baseball players. The average fan can look to the body of work of a player and shake their head at how pitiful their performance was, how they barely broke through to the big leagues, wallowed in obscurity, or perhaps squandered unlimited potential or media hype by falling on their face. As a rule we remember the stars and their great accomplishments, but the average players, the scrubs, and the wannabes come and go and become the stuff of trivia questions and nostalgic fan memories. But for every rule there are exceptions. Horace Clarke was an average player, perhaps even a notch above average. Rather than being forgotten, they named an entire era of Yankee history after him. The Horace Clarke Era is the term commonly used by baseball fans and historians to describe the dreadful period between the Yankees' World Series trip in 1964 and the beginning of the George Steinbrenner Era. Unfortunately, the choice of Clarke as the icon of mediocrity was both unfair and oddly inappropriate; unfair because Clarke was as good or better than many of the second basemen that he played against, and unfair because he was one of the few Yankees talented enough to hold a starting position throughout most of the period that he came to represent.

Horace Clarke's path to immortality was rather remarkable. Born in 1940 in the United States Virgin Islands, where cricket was often the sport of choice over baseball, Clarke's success ranks second only to NBA great Tim Duncan among the territory's native-born professional athletes. Clarke was signed to a contract by the Yankees in 1958, just three years after Elston Howard became the first person of color to play a regular season game for the club. Clarke toiled for eight years in the Yankee minor league system, beginning his professional life as a shortstop before sliding over to second base in his seventh year as a pro. Clarke established his reputation as a durable speedster who rarely struck out. He was a productive hitter, batting over .300 three times with additional .292 and .299 seasons to his credit. He proved his ability to play at every level of the minors before stalling out at the AAA level, the highest level of minor league baseball. Blocked from progression to the major league club by a group of young infielders like Clete Boyer, Tony Kubek, Bobby Richardson, Phil Linz, Bobby Murcer, and Pedro Gonzalez, Clarke ended up spending two and a half years at the AAA level before getting the call to join the big club in May of 1965 when the Yankees traded Gonzalez to the Indians. It must be noted that when Clarke made his debut on May 13, the Yankees were in eighth place in a ten-team league. Apparently the Horace Clarke Era had begun before the man it was named for had even played an inning with the team. He spent two months with the Yankees, pinch hitting and filling in around the infield as needed, returned to AAA for two months in the summer, and returned to the Yankees to stay when the rosters expanded in September. Clarke performed solidly as a utility infielder and pinch hitter for the second half of 1965 and set himself up for a more prominent role on the team for the following season.

Clarke's future prospects took a turn for the better after the 1965 season when star infielders Tony Kubek and Bobby Richardson each announced their retirement, Kubek for health reasons and Richardson to spend time at home with his family. Both were only twenty-nine years old. Clarke was already tagged to assume the second base role when the Yankees convinced Richardson to delay his departure for one year while the club trained his replacement. Richardson agreed, and the twenty-six year-old Clarke became Richardson's apprentice. Clarke spent the first half of the dreadful 1966 season on the bench as Richardson's understudy, reprising his role as a pinch hitter and utility man from the previous season before assuming the job of everyday shortstop as an emergency stopgap in July. When Richardson made it clear to the front office that his mind was made up and the 1966 season would be his last, Clarke moved to his new home at second base in late September. It was a home that he would own without challenge for the next seven seasons.

During his seven seasons as the everyday Yankee second baseman Horace Clarke averaged 151 games, leading the club in stolen bases four times. His .256 career batting average was remarkably consistent year over year and was enough to assure him a spot at the top of the Yankee batting order. His most glaring weakness was his defense, and he developed a reputation for shying away from incoming runners, limiting his effectiveness at turning the double play and drawing the wrath of the pitching staff. Still, he was a solid fixture at a position that was not known at that time for producing star players. In fact, of the ten American League starting second basemen on the job when Clarke assumed the role in 1967, only Clarke, Hall of Famer Rod Carew, Dick McAuliffe, and Dick Green still held the starting role at that position for their original teams entering the 1973 season. The Horace Clarke Era was hardly a golden age of second basemen across the American League.

Yankee Resurrection

Yankee fans could have interpreted Clarke's presence on the field every day as a symbol of gritty, grind-it-out determination, a relatively average athlete making the most of his abilities, showing up every day giving everything he had in an often losing effort. Instead, that same consistency worked against him. Year after year you could count on Horace Clarke to provide average performance. Year after year you could count on the New York Yankees to provide average performance. The two seemed to go together. Yankee fans had grown frustrated with the club's acceptance of Horace Clarke as the only answer at second base. The fact that the shortstop position had been in a similar rut since Gene Michael assumed the everyday role there in 1969 only exacerbated the issue. The perceived lack of performance in the two middle infield positions, amplified by management's seeming unwillingness to upgrade either position as each postseason passed by, had become "Exhibit A" in what was seen as front office indifference and acceptance of the status quo. And like many things in the Steinbrenner Era, this too had to change.

Gabe Paul made his intentions to upgrade his team's middle infield quite clear as he went into the winter meetings in December. Both Gene Michael and Horace Clarke, used to criticism by the fans, rankled under the lack of confidence publicly shown by their management. Michael was particularly vocal, defending his record and blaming the knock on the tandem's defense on the poor quality of the Yankee Stadium infield surface. Michael's protest did him no good, as the Yankees purchased Jim Mason from Texas on December 6, 1973. The Yankees continued the search for top flight middle infielders, but when none were found they announced that the shortstop and second base jobs would be won through an open competition between the existing candidates at the spring camp in March. Jim Mason was the early favorite at the shortstop position, a role that he cemented in Florida. Candidates for the second base job included the unpopular incumbent Clarke, the displaced Gene Michael, and the duo of Fred Stanley and Billy Parker, two players who has bounced between the major and minor leagues for the past few seasons. Clarke damaged what remaining chance he had of retaining his old job when he refused to sign a contract and left Yankee training camp on March 4. Gabe Paul invoked an automatic contract renewal option, and Clarke realized that if he wanted to continue his baseball career he had no choice but to accept the terms and return to camp to fight for his job. The odds were stacked against him from the start, and when the club broke camp Clarke found himself on the bench for the first time in eight years. In an ironic twist of fate, it was teammate Gene Michael who won the second base job. Neither Mason nor Michael received much of a vote of confidence from the front office, as Gabe Paul candidly announced his strong desire to acquire a middle infielder who could contribute more offensively, even as the 1974 season opened.

While Mason cemented his hold on the shortstop position with steady defense and sufficient, if barely acceptable, offense, Michael's reign as the Yankee starting second baseman ended after less than a month with the thirty-six year-old veteran's batting average sitting at a miniscule .125. The job had been his to lose and he lost it. In desperation the Yankees turned back to Clarke, who returned to his former role as starting second baseman. His comeback lasted a grand total of six games. Despite a .263 batting average, Clarke carried too much of a stigma to hold the job for long. On May 5 the team purchased Fernando Gonzalez from Kansas City, and he immediately replaced Clarke. Gonzalez had been an outstanding minor league player, but as his .235 lifetime major league batting average shows he never quite translated that to success at the upper level. Moreover, he was a third baseman by trade, with relatively little experience at second. Still, the Horace Clarke Era had to end and Gonzalez was handed the job. Clarke returned to the bench, relegated to infrequent appearances on the playing field. On May 22 Clarke returned to the starting lineup as leadoff hitter and second baseman for the very last time in pinstripes. A little more than a week later on May 31, Horace Clarke was traded to the cellar-dwelling San Diego Padres for pitcher Lowell Palmer. It was a trade of two unwanted, excess parts – Palmer would never again appear in a major league game, while Clarke would ride the bench in San Diego before being released in October, ending his professional baseball career.

The end of the Horace Clarke Era, though welcomed by many fans ignorant of the decent contributions made by a man who was widely liked by his teammates, did not end without some controversy. Clarke's exile from the Yankee organization came with little more than a phone call and a plane ticket. Despite having spent seventeen years with the organization, nobody from that organization saw fit to wish him well and thank him for his efforts. Public relations executive Marty Appel, a decent man in a difficult role, tried unsuccessfully to say "Goodbye" to Clarke on behalf of the organization before he left.

In one single transaction, the trade of Horace Clarke represented both a further break from an intolerable period of Yankee mediocrity and a manifestation of the cold-heartedness of the new management team. It was yet another symbol of the changes taking place in the Yankee organization.

May 31, 1974	W	L	PCT	GB
Milwaukee Brewers	24	20	.545	-
Boston Red Sox	25	22	.532	0.5
Baltimore Orioles	22	24	.478	3
Detroit Tigers	22	24	.478	3
Cleveland Indians	22	25	.468	3.5
New York Yankees	23	27	.460	4

The Last Champion

The biomechanical motion of throwing a baseball is acknowledged as being one of the most unnatural actions that the human body can perform. The stress and strain of that activity puts enormous pressure on the body, particularly the shoulder and elbow joints. The state of medical science in 1974 was such that healthcare professionals and baseball pitching coaches were entering a new era of understanding of the injury risks and treatment options. The science of understanding the biomechanics of pitching and creating new methods for the treatment of injuries came together in 1974 in the city of Los Angles, home of the Dodgers. The centerpieces of the Dodger pitching staff were Tommy John, anchor of the starting pitching rotation, and Mike Marshall, the premier relief pitcher in the game. In addition to being among the game's elite pitchers, Marshall was an expert in the science of kinesiology, the study of body motion. Marshall had incorporated his academic knowledge of the subject into a revolutionary program that influenced his pitching motion, his pickoff move, and his physical preparation and recovery. Marshall would pitch a mind-boggling and record-setting 106 games on his way to a Cy Young award in 1974. Five years later Marshall was still at it, pitching in a remarkable ninety games at the age of thirty-six. While Marshall was setting records for durability, teammate Tommy John was on a different path. At the age of thirty-one and a veteran of twelve major league seasons, by July John was enjoying the very best season of his career when he faced the Montreal Expos on the evening of July 17. Pitching with a record of 13-3 and a four run lead in the third inning, John was forced to leave the game with a sore elbow. John's injury was diagnosed as a torn Ulnar Collateral Ligament. There was no established treatment for a torn UCL in 1974 – it was a career death sentence, particularly for a thirty-one year-old pitcher. But Dr. Frank Jobe, a member of the Dodger medical staff, proposed performing an experimental surgical procedure to reconstruct the elbow by replacing the torn UCL with a tendon from John's leg. A little more than two months after the injury, Tommy John underwent the surgery that would later bear his name. John resumed his spot on the mound and among the game's elite pitchers in 1976 in a recovery that was widely hailed as a medical miracle. In the decades to come, Tommy John Surgery would become so commonplace and so effective that athletes would not only embrace the procedure but would sometimes seek it out as a discretionary, preventative measure. But despite these breakthroughs, cases of career-ending injuries among professional pitchers were prevalent and pitchers knew that the tragic end of a pitching career could be just a pitch away. The rotator cuff, a group of muscles and tendons in the shoulder joint, was a particularly sensitive part of a pitcher's anatomy, and there were no effective surgical or rehabilitative treatments available for the most serious rotator cuff injuries. No pitcher and no team was immune from career-ending arm injuries, as the Yankees and their fans would sadly witness.

By June Mel Stottlemyre was the lone remaining Yankee on the active roster who had played for the team during their last championship season in 1964. The recently departed Mike Hegan had a cup of coffee with the 1964 club and had benefitted from late season injuries to Tony Kubek and Jake Gibbs to secure a spot on that year's World Series roster. But after bouncing between AAA and the Yankees for the next four years, the Yankees gave up on Hegan and sent him off to a reasonably productive career with the Pilots, Brewers, and Athletics before reacquiring him in late 1973. Gabe Paul had made it quite clear that Hegan was not a long-term solution at first base and the acquisition of Chris Chambliss made it even clearer than ever that Hegan did not fit into the Yankees plans. For two weeks after the Chambliss deal Hegan saw his playing time reduced to a single pinch hitting appearance. After waiting impatiently for the Yankees to send him elsewhere Hegan finally forced the issue, threatening to quit if he was not dealt immediately. The Yankees gladly acquiesced, and Hegan was sent to the Milwaukee Brewers in mid-May. His departure left Mel Stottlemyre as the sole remaining link to the Yankees glory years.

The home-grown Stottlemyre had risen rapidly through the Yankee farm system, posting outstanding results in two full and two partial minor league seasons. With their backs against the wall in August of 1964, the Yankees brought Mel up to the big club and inserted him in the starting rotation in place of Stan Williams and Roland Sheldon. Many players before and since would wither in the glare of the New York spotlight, but if the pressure of pitching in an intense pennant race bothered the twenty-two year-old he did not show it. Stottlemyre was widely praised for stabilizing the Yankee starting rotation and he won nine out of twelve decisions down the stretch, sporting a dazzling 2.06 ERA and earning votes in the Most Valuable Player balloting. Stottlemyre's magical rookie season culminated with the honor of starting the seventh game of the 1964 World Series against the legendary Bob Gibson, the third start in the series for Stottlemyre. While the rookie performed well in the biggest spotlight in sports, he was outmatched by Gibson and was the losing pitcher in what would be the last Yankee World Series game for over a decade.

Stottlemyre proved that his debut season was no fluke by defying the sophomore jinx and winning twenty games and leading the league in complete games and innings pitched in his first full season in 1965. His fortunes reversed in parallel with the Yankees decline in 1966 as he racked up twenty losses while the team finished in tenth place. After his nineteenth loss that painful season, Ralph Houk removed him from the starting rotation to save him from the potential indignity of losing twenty games. The move backfired when Houk unwisely inserted Stottlemyre in relief in an extra inning game on the last weekend of the season and Mel gave up the winning run and was subsequently charged with his twentieth loss.

For the next seven seasons Stottlemyre solidified his position as the ace of the Yankee staff and for a time as one of the best pitchers in the game. Over nine full seasons from 1965-1973 Mel averaged 16.5 wins per season, highlighted by his selection as the starting pitcher in the 1969 All-Star Game as a last minute replacement for Denny McLain. Stottlemyre also earned the reputation as a workhorse as the five-time All-Star averaged almost 275 innings pitched per year during that same period, twice leading the league in complete games.

By the 1970s Stottlemyre was still the consensus ace of the Yankee pitching staff, but his performance reflected the years of stress that he had been putting on his right arm. His right shoulder was feeling the strain of the thousands of pitches he had thrown, and he required cortisone treatments, the standard of care for such injuries at that time, and experimental x-ray therapy just to be able to begin a new season. Stottlemyre's performance began to decline, though he demonstrated a remarkable ability to answer the call and take his place on the mound without complaining about the pain or missing time due to injury. He led the American League in losses with eighteen in 1972, although he rebounded to lead the Yankee staff in wins in 1973 when he posted a 16-16 record. Stottlemyre's long-term performance and his stature with the Yankees had made him one of the highest-paid pitchers in the game with a $90,000 annual salary. It was this statistic that perhaps above all others made Mel stand out in the eyes of the new Yankee management team, a fact that would have severe consequences in the days to come.

Stottlemyre was the Yankee starting pitcher on Opening Day of 1974, a role that he had ably filled for seven of the past eight seasons. For the first two and a half months of the season the thirty-two year-old Stottlemyre performed much as he had through the previous ten seasons – he showed up on the mound every fourth or fifth day and generally kept the Yankees in the game. By the time of his start against the Angels at Shea Stadium on June 11 he had completed six of his fourteen starts, including his last two, and had allowed more than four earned runs only once all year. In the four starts leading up to June 11 he had accumulated thirty-four innings pitched. To the casual observer, Mel Stottlemyre's durability seemed unquestioned.

On that June night Stottlemyre got into trouble in the second inning – a walk, a couple of singles, a wild pitch, and he was down 3-0. In the top of the third he was pitching to Frank Robinson when he reached for a little something extra in an attempt to close out Robinson's at bat. He got Robinson to fly out for the third out, but in the process heard a pop and felt a searing pain "like a lightning bolt" in his pitching shoulder. He returned to the mound to start the next inning but after surrendering a home run and a single he left the mound in agony.

Stottlemyre was placed on the disabled list for the first time in his career. With the state-of-the-art in sports medicine and the diagnosis and treatment of severe shoulder injuries still their infancy, the initial diagnosis was a muscle tear and rest was seen as the only viable treatment. Stottlemyre rested on the sidelines for almost two months. He returned to the mound in a relief appearance on August 4, ending his American League record streak for most games started without pitching in relief. He threw ineffectively for two innings and his shoulder did not show any evidence of recovery. After making an appearance as a pinch runner two weeks later, Mel Stottlemyre returned to the disabled list. For Stottlemyre, the 1974 season was over.

With four pitchers shipped off to Cleveland and Mel Stottlemyre effectively finished for the year, the Yankee pitching staff which had looked so deep in spring training was now in a very precarious position.

June 11, 1974	W	L	PCT	GB
Boston Red Sox	32	25	.561	-
Milwaukee Brewers	28	25	.528	2
Cleveland Indians	28	27	.509	3
Detroit Tigers	28	28	.500	3.5
New York Yankees	29	31	.483	4.5
Baltimore Orioles	27	29	.482	4.5

The Rotation

The standard starting pitching model was the same in 1974 as it had been for decades – four men, each pitching with three days of rest, would hold a spot in the rotation as long as their health and their performance allowed them to. They would pitch, rest a day, throw on the sidelines or perhaps in a brief relief situation on the second day, rest again on the third day, and return to the mound for another start on the fourth day. This routine would only be interrupted by a strategically placed day off, which might allow a club to skip over their fourth starter, or a double header, which often required the service of a fifth starter. The 1966 Dodgers won a National League pennant by covering the entire 162 game season with only five starters – the four-man rotation of Sandy Koufax, Don Drysdale, Claude Osteen, and Don Sutton, and occasional fifth starter Joe Moeller. Moeller would start only eight games, five of which were part of double headers. The Dodger starting four even managed to work three relief appearances into their heavy workload.

The 1974 Yankees confidently followed the four-man rotation standard. Though they would go on to play fifteen double headers over the course of the season, the club was confident that they had the depth to handle the load. With Peterson in the doghouse and on the trading block, the team opened the year with Mel Stottlemyre, Doc Medich, Pat Dobson, and Steve Kline handling starting duties, with Peterson and Sam McDowell filling in when a fifth starter was required. New Yankee Dick Tidrow arrived from Cleveland and immediately settled into Kline's slot in the rotation. The spot starter role was a different story. Peterson was now wearing an Indians uniform. McDowell had become a source of major frustration. His performance declined significantly, culminating with a late May relief appearance in which he came into a game with the bases loaded and proceeded to walk three hitters, scoring all three inherited runners. The poor performance was blamed on a slipped disc, which landed McDowell on the disabled list. The lefty's behavior off the field continued to reflect his ongoing battle with alcohol (McDowell later admitted the back injury originally occurred when he fell after a night drinking at a nightclub). The trade of Peterson and injury to McDowell had drained the pool of available left handed starters and had left the pitching staff without a much needed spot starter. On May 4 the club acquired Dick Woodson from the Twins for minor leaguer Mike Pazik. A year shy of thirty, Woodson was an imposing presence on the mound and had performed admirably for the Twins as a starting pitcher, but by the time of his arrival at Shea he was damaged goods due to a serious arm injury that would effectively end his career. Woodson would start the nightcaps of three double headers, pitching progressively worse in each outing. Stottlemyre lookalike Dave Pagan was recalled from the minor leagues to help carry the load, but Pagan wasn't ready for big league competition. Although the starters were generally keeping games close, only Doc Medich had a winning record when Stottlemyre went down from his injury. The pitching staff was already starting to be stretched thin when Stottlemyre was injured, and with the loss of their ace there was now another hole to fill. With a lineup that still featured a hole at second base and sub-par performances from at least three other positions, things were not looking good for the Yankees as the trade deadline approached. Gabe Paul was running out of options and running out of time, and Yankee fans were running out of patience.

June 15, 1974	W	L	PCT	GB
Boston Red Sox	34	26	.567	-
Cleveland Indians	30	28	.517	3
Baltimore Orioles	30	29	.508	3.5
Detroit Tigers	30	29	.508	3.5
New York Yankees	31	32	.492	4.5
Milwaukee Brewers	28	29	.491	4.5

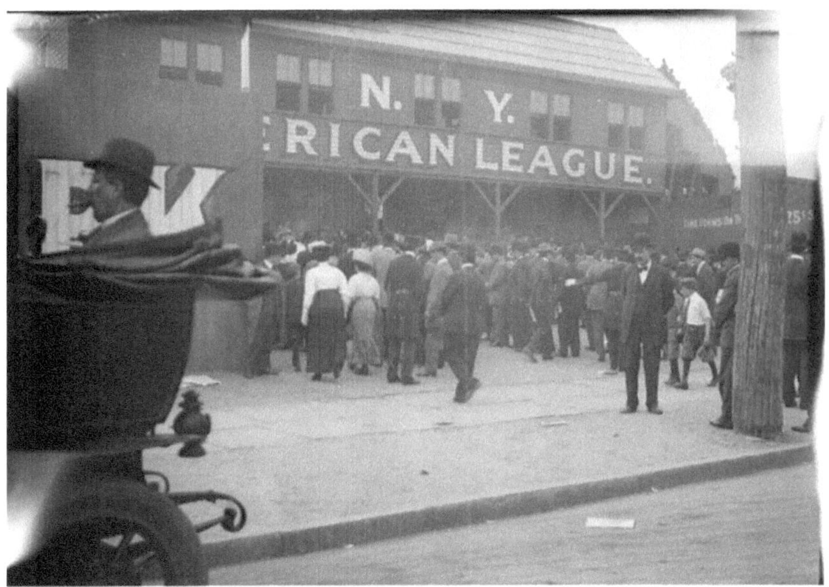

American League Park, more commonly known as Hilltop Park, sat at the heights of upper Manhattan and served as the first home of the American League's New York franchise from 1903-1912. In honor of their locale the home team adopted Highlanders as their nickname until the team moved to the newly rebuilt Polo Grounds and adopted the legendary Yankee nickname in 1913. The wooden ballpark was built in just a few weeks and was not completely finished when the Highlanders opened their 1903 season.

Library of Congress, Prints & Photographs Division, [LC-B21- 2186-13]

Ground was broken for Yankee Stadium on May 5, 1922. This state-of-the-art edifice, later tagged by New York sports personality Art Rust Jr. as "The Big Ball Orchard in the Bronx," was built from the ground up in less than a year. The architect was Osborn Engineering, who designed many of the famous sports stadiums in the 20th Century. Like future Yankee owner George Steinbrenner, Osborn made their home in Cleveland, Ohio. The Yankees played their first game in their new home on April 18, 1923 and Babe Ruth christened the new stadium with a third inning home run. The stadium would play host to the first of many World Series games six months later.

This version of Yankee Stadium would be the home of the Yankees through the 1973 season, after which the ballpark was closed for two years of renovations that forced the Yankees across town to Shea Stadium for the 1974-1975 seasons.

U.S. Department of the Interior, National Park Service, Edison National Historic Site
Library of Congress, Prints & Photographs Division, [LC-B2- 5958-11]

The newly organized Yankee management team in spring 1973. From left to right, Ralph Houk, George Steinbrenner, Gabe Paul, Lee MacPhail, and Mike Burke. The contrast in style between Burke and Steinbrenner is clear from their appearance, and note the fact that Burke seems to be the only member of the group whose attention lies elsewhere as he looks into the distance. Burke, Houk, and MacPhail would all be gone by the end of the year.

A career as a war hero, secret agent, circus manager, and broadcasting executive preceded Michael Burke's reign as President and CEO of the New York Yankees. Even that diverse background and wartime exploits that earned him a Silver Star, Navy Cross, and the French Médaille de la Résistance did not prepare Burke for a partnership with George Steinbrenner.

National Baseball Hall of Fame and Museum, Cooperstown, NY

George M. Steinbrenner III headed a diverse and high-powered team of investors who purchased the Yankees from CBS prior to the 1973 season. Determined to remake the classic Yankee franchise in his own image, the new principal owner was disinterested in Yankee traditions that he considered an encumbrance to immediate success. Players, field management, and front office staff would soon feel the pressure of an owner desperate for victory and willing to do anything for a championship.
National Baseball Hall of Fame and Museum, Cooperstown, NY

Yankee Resurrection

Lee MacPhail's philosophy as a general manager prioritized the patient development of home grown talent over the importation of players through trades. That formula worked well for MacPhail during his time with the Baltimore Orioles, but his years with the Yankees were marked by mediocre performance. MacPhail's steady, patient style immediately conflicted with the "win now" personality of George Steinbrenner, leading to MacPhail's departure after one season under the new owner.

National Baseball Hall of Fame and Museum, Cooperstown, NY

Gabe Paul was a baseball lifer who worked his way up through the ranks from minor league batboy to President of the New York Yankees. "The Smiling Cobra" employed a two-pronged offensive of overwhelming charm and vicious tactics to get what he wanted. Hand-picked by new owner George Steinbrenner to run the baseball operations of the Yankees, Paul reflected Steinbrenner's impatient style and he became the key architect in the rebuilding of the Yankee roster.

National Baseball Hall of Fame and Museum, Cooperstown, NY

A late season photo of the 1973 New York Yankees, the first Yankee team to play under the Steinbrenner regime. The club initially consisted of players inherited by the new ownership team, but within a year many of these players would be gone as the new management embarked upon a major rebuilding effort. Well over half of the uniformed personnel in this photo who had survived the first season under George Steinbrenner would be gone a year later.

Front row (L-R): Roy White, Horace Clarke, Elston Howard (Coach), Jim Turner (Coach), Ralph Houk (Manager), Jim Hegan (Coach), Dick Howser (Coach), Matty Alou, Bobby Murcer, Jerry Moses.

Second row (L-R): Gene Monahan (Trainer) Mike Hegan, Jim Ray Hart, Thurman Munson, Graig Nettles, Fred Stanley, Ron Blomberg, Celerino Sanchez, Felipe Alou, Gene Michael, Pete Sheehy (Equipment Mgr), Rob Franklin (Traveling Sec)

Top row (L-R): Fritz Peterson, Mel Stottlemyre, Hal Lanier, Wayne Granger, Steve Kline, Pat Dobson, Lindy McDaniel, George "Doc" Medich, Sam McDowell, Tom Buskey, Sparky Lyle, Fred Beene.

Seated: Kevin Melchoir and Gerry Murphy (Batboys)

National Baseball Hall of Fame and Museum, Cooperstown, NY

Yankee Resurrection

The United States Army and the New York Yankees were the only two organizations that baseball lifer Ralph Houk had ever worked for when George Steinbrenner took over the Yankees. Accustomed to a completely free hand in running the ballclub, the Major chafed under the shadow of Steinbrenner and resented the new owner's public criticism of his ballplayers. The mounting pressure on Houk resulted in his resignation as Yankee manager on the last day of the 1973 season after one year as a Steinbrenner employee.

National Baseball Hall of Fame and Museum, Cooperstown, NY

"The Home of the Mets is honored to house the
New York Yankees, and we will all be rooting for
you until we meet in the subway World Series of
1974!"

Sincerely,

Bill

William A. Shea

In 1974 Yankee fans were welcomed to their temporary home at Shea
Stadium by the stadium's namesake, Bill Shea. Meanwhile, their true home
ballpark underwent a massive, two-year reconstruction.

Bill Virdon knew that he was not George Steinbrenner's first choice to manage the Yankees, but still accepted the role when Steinbrenner was unable to negotiate the release of Dick Williams from Charles O. Finley and the Oakland Athletics. A polar opposite in many ways to Ralph Houk, Virdon overcame a rocky relationship with many of his Yankee players to lead the team to their best finish in a decade.
National Baseball Hall of Fame and Museum, Cooperstown, NY

The period from 1965-1973 is derisively known in Yankee circles as the "Horace Clarke Era." This unkind notoriety fell upon a steady performing infielder who served the Yankees well for almost a decade. Clarke was a symbol of Yankee ineptitude in the eyes of the Steinbrenner front office, and he found himself on the bench and ultimately out the door as the 1974 season progressed.

National Baseball Hall of Fame and Museum, Cooperstown, NY

Bobby Murcer carried the Yankee lineup after the retirement of the beloved Mickey Mantle in 1969. The wildly popular Murcer thrived in the spotlight and took his place among the top players in baseball from 1969-1973. The move to Shea Stadium and the unrelenting pressure of high expectations by Gabe Paul and George Steinbrenner led to trouble on the field for Murcer in 1974 and ultimately paved the way for his exile from the Yankees.
National Baseball Hall of Fame and Museum, Cooperstown, NY

Thurman Munson earned a permanent spot in the hearts of Yankee fans with his ability as a ballplayer and his gritty, no-nonsense approach to the game of baseball. The star catcher held a unique distinction of being wildly popular with fans, teammates, and even Yankee owner George Steinbrenner, so much so that the iconoclastic Steinbrenner broke with tradition to make Munson the first captain of the Yankees since the retirement of Lou Gehrig.

National Baseball Hall of Fame and Museum, Cooperstown, NY

As trades and injuries depleted the 1974 Yankee pitching staff, Pat Dobson (left) and George "Doc" Medich (right) filled the void to win a combined total of thirty-eight games in 1974. The righty duo kept the Yankees in the pennant race throughout the 1974 season.

National Baseball Hall of Fame and Museum, Cooperstown, NY

No player represents the transitional nature of the 1974 New York Yankees better than Elliott Maddox. Acquired as a backup prior to the season, the outfielder parleyed a stellar glove into an everyday role in the Yankee lineup. After displacing the popular Bobby Murcer from center field, Maddox went on to have a career-best season in the field and at the plate.

National Baseball Hall of Fame and Museum, Cooperstown, NY

By August of 1974 the roster of the Band on the Run Yankees had largely been set. Pitcher Larry Gura would join the club shortly after this photo was taken, completing the roster that would lead the Yankees into the September stretch drive.

Front row (L-R): Roy White, Sandy Alomar, Elston Howard (Coach), Mel Wright (Coach), Bill Virdon (Manager), Dick Howser (Coach), Whitey Ford (Coach), Bobby Murcer, Elliott Maddox, Lou Piniella, Walt Williams

Second row (L-R): Gene Monahan (Trainer), Jim Mason, Rick Dempsey, Chris Chambliss, Otto Velez, Rudy May, Ron Blomberg, Gene Michael, Dave Pagan, Graig Nettles, Pete Sheehy (Equip Mgr), Bill Kane (Traveling Sec)

Top row (L-R): Bill Sudakis, Mike Wallace, Pat Dobson, Sparky Lyle, George "Doc" Medich, Sam McDowell, Cecil Upshaw, Mel Stottlemyre, Dick Tidrow, Thurman Munson

Seated on the ground: Unidentified batboys

National Baseball Hall of Fame and Museum, Cooperstown, NY

The year 1976 saw the return of the Yankees to their newly renovated home and the return of World Series baseball to Yankee Stadium.

PART THREE

BAND ON THE RUN

Rallying Cry

The New York Yankees weren't the only iconic brand trying to revitalize its image in the 1970s.

Paul McCartney began his solo career a short time before the public announcement of the dissolution of the Beatles in April 1970. His first project highlighted his desire to move away from the sophisticated and elaborate production elements of the later Beatle recordings in favor of a minimalistic approach to arranging and recording. As McCartney began to find his footing as a solo artist, his devoted fans bought his new material in impressive amounts while critics took a more negative view, characterizing his new work as thin and uneven at best. Subsequent recordings followed a similar pattern, and despite a steady trend toward more sophisticated production and higher quality material, the critics continued to hold the former Beatle to a high standard and persisted in their harsh reviews of his work. McCartney's estranged former songwriting partner and bandmate John Lennon offered perhaps the harshest assessment of McCartney's post-Beatles output by using his song "How Do You Sleep?" to contrast the content of McCartney's Beatle classic "Yesterday" with his solo hit "Another Day" with the scathing line "The only thing you done was yesterday and since you're gone you're just another day."

After his first two solo projects McCartney reinvented himself through the framework of a new band called Wings, a moniker later adjusted to the more commercially compelling Paul McCartney and

Wings. Two more projects under the Wings banner followed, but while record sales remained solid the critics were still not appeased.

It was in this set of circumstances that McCartney created the third album under the Wings name. *"Band on the Run"* distinguished itself from its predecessors by drawing widespread praise from critics while also capturing the hearts of music fans, who rewarded McCartney's efforts by buying over three million copies of the album. The album's title track was released as the album's second single, and in April 1974 it reached the top of the U.S. singles chart. Freedom from past business decisions gone wrong inspired songwriter McCartney to write a set of lyrics around the theme of breaking out of a virtual prison and enjoying the excitement of life on the run, confounding those who would seek to recapture him. The concept of a band of renegades merrily tweaking the establishment found a receptive ear in the listening public, including the occupants of the New York Yankee clubhouse.

One of the most valuable pieces of equipment in the clubhouse of the 1974 New York Yankees had nothing at all to do with baseball. It was not used by the training staff. It wasn't even supplied by the team. The most valuable piece of equipment in the clubhouse was an eight track tape player owned by Bill Sudakis.

Bill Sudakis was a colorful character with many sides. One beat reporter referred to him as "a candidate for the 'Good Guy Award' on any club," while another noted that a conversation with Sudakis featured "enough bleeps to make the director of an X-rated movie turn blue." His professional baseball track record was equally complicated. Signed in 1964 as an eighteen year-old infielder by the highly respected Los Angeles Dodgers organization, Sudakis slowly worked his way through the talent-rich Dodger farm system to finally make his Los Angeles debut as the Dodger "third baseman of the future" in September of 1968. Sudakis held the starting third base job through the 1969 season, during which he impressed observers with his power from both sides of the plate but showed relatively few other noteworthy skills. With emerging talent like Steve Garvey available, the Dodgers concluded that Sudakis had no future as an everyday player and convinced him that his best option for remaining in the major leagues was to become a utility player. Sudakis was given the opportunity to spend time in the Arizona Fall League to learn to catch, and from that point forward Bill Sudakis was stuck with the title "switch-hitting utility man." Sudakis spent the next season and a half splitting time between catcher, first and third base, and the outfield, posting an impressively high home run percentage but doing little to secure a full time job at any one position. His career took a serious turn for the worse in June of 1971 when a collision at home plate resulted in a serious knee injury. The Dodgers cut Sudakis loose the following spring, and after one injury-riddled season with the New York Mets Sudakis found himself in Texas for the 1973 season. It was while with the Rangers that Sudakis resurrected his career, reprising the utility role that he had carved out with the Dodgers while hitting a career high fifteen home runs. After the cash-strapped Rangers sold Sudakis to the Yankees, new manager Billy Martin publicly expressed his disappointment with losing such a hard-working and versatile player and unsuccessfully lobbied for the Ranger management team to get him back. Sudakis settled into the role of part time player with the Yankees, mostly appearing as the designated hitter with occasional appearances at first base.

While Sudakis played a supporting role in the lineup he was playing a much more important role in the clubhouse. Sudakis and teammate Elliott Maddox referred to each other as "bandits," and under that persona Sudakis immediately took to McCartney's "Band on the Run." Sudakis played the tune over and over again on his clubhouse boom box, and soon the song was a rallying cry for the ball club. Marty Appel of the Yankee public relations team, a fan of McCartney and The Beatles, picked up on what was happening and soon "Band on the Run" could be regularly heard on the Shea Stadium public address system and the club's radio broadcasts. Even the club's press notes began referring to the Yankees as the Band on the Run.

While the front office and the fans in the seats grew impatient with the club's mediocre showing in the standings, the confidence of the ballplayers themselves began to skyrocket, fueled by their self-branded persona as the renegade outlaws of the American League east. The team was loose, they were confident, and they were having fun. Despite a lackluster first half performance, an infectious attitude of positivity prevailed in the Yankee clubhouse. The Band on the Run Yankees believed in themselves, even if nobody else did. They just needed time to jell and to find a way to fill the remaining gaps on their roster.

Heavenly Help

Nothing had come easy in Rudy May's professional baseball career. Signed by the Minnesota Twins prior to the 1963 season, he would already be a journeyman by the time he reached the majors in 1965 at the age of twenty. After one year as property of the Twins, the young lefthander was drafted by the Chicago White Sox. After one minor league season in the Chicago organization he was traded to the Phillies, who in turn traded him to the Angels just a few weeks later. By the time he reported to spring training with the Angels in 1965 he had already been the property of four teams with only two seasons in the low minors to show for it. On the basis of his minor league performance and given the lack of talent on the Angels' pitching staff, May earned a spot in the Angel starting rotation in 1965, posting an unimpressive 4-9 record for the season. Three years of exile in the Angel minor league system followed, leading to a return to the big club in 1969. May held a regular spot in the Angels weak pitching rotation for the next five years with a disappointing 47-67 record. By 1974 the team had lost patience with him, and though he held on to a tenuous spot on the roster he found himself banished to the bullpen, doing a poor job in a mop-up role that seemed to signal the coming end of his career.

Then came salvation, in the form of a ticket to New York.

The Yankees, desperate to fill the hole left by the loss of Mel Stottlemyre and without seeing a viable option within their own organization, once again looked outside of the organization for help. With only three healthy starters remaining, and with all of them being right-handed, Gabe Paul looked far and wide for a capable left-handed starter to plug the gap. With pitching in short supply around the major leagues, Paul settled on Rudy May, acquiring the lefty at the trade deadline on June 15. Whether a stroke of luck or a stroke of genius, the move immediately paid off. Returning to a starting role, and backed by a solid defense and a decent lineup, May flourished. After spending a week on the bullpen bench, May assumed Stottlemyre's spot in the rotation on June 23. He proceeded to rattle off three straight complete games, giving up only four earned runs and fourteen hits in twenty-six innings of work. After the failure of Ken Wright, Rick Sawyer, Dick Woodson, and Dave Pagan, the Yankees believed they had finally struck gold with May. Good performances are contagious, and Rudy May was just what the doctor ordered for the Yankee pitching staff. The man that the cellar-dwelling Angels cast off had become the savior of the Yankee starting rotation.

Despite the cause for optimism infused by the strong performance of Rudy May, the pennant hopes of the Yankees remained relatively dim as their season reached its halfway point. On June 19 the team was a game over .500 but then proceeded to lose nine out of their next ten with the only win coming courtesy of May. By the midway point the Yankees were not only in last place, but it seemed like every team in the division but the Yankees had enjoyed the opportunity to have their day in the sun at the top of the division. Fortunately, nobody had yet put together a sustained hot streak that enabled them to pull away from the rest of the pack, so the Yankees' chances were still theoretically good. Yankee Manager Bill Virdon predicted that ninety-one wins would be enough to take the division. Virdon's theory was supported by the fact that the Cleveland Indians, temporary occupants of the first place slot at mid-season, had won forty-five games. If Virdon's prediction were to be true the club had a serious math problem to contend with. After half a season, the Yankees winning percentage stood at a mediocre .469. Achievement of Virdon's ninety-one win target would require the team to win almost two-thirds of their remaining games, and the rest of the division would need to cooperate by refraining from getting hot and running away with the top spot. The latter was not likely. Boston was clearly building the core of a very good club, one that would be a major force in the second half of the decade. Baltimore, having won four of the last five divisional championships, always loomed large. Even the first-place Indians were showing signs of being capable of winning the division. With so many ex-teammates now playing for Cleveland, Bobby Murcer launched one of his most famous sarcastic jibes against the new Yankee management, quipping that if the Yanks kept shipping players to Cleveland "pretty soon they would have a very good club." Worse still, there was little about the first half performance of the 1974 Yankees that foreshadowed any hope that the club could turn things around and start to suddenly win games at the rate necessary to hit Virdon's ninety-one win target. The Yankees seemed destined to finish yet another season in the bottom half of the standings. But through the works of George Steinbrenner, Gabe Paul, and Bill Virdon, this Yankee team was not anything like their predecessors who had run out of gas midway through the year only to cruise to the finish line.

The Yankees, their fans, and their impatient owner and general manager were about to go on a wild ride.

July 3, 1974	W	L	PCT	GB
Boston Red Sox	43	34	.558	-
Cleveland Indians	42	34	.553	0.5
Detroit Tigers	41	36	.532	2
Baltimore Orioles	40	36	.526	2.5
Milwaukee Brewers	36	39	.480	6
New York Yankees	35	42	.455	8

Role Player

By July 12 Elliott Maddox was still demonstrating that his early success in the field and at the plate was no fluke. His batting average rose above .300 on the first of June, never to fall below that level again in 1974. On July 12 he entered the game against the Oakland Athletics hitting .330 while also playing at a Gold Glove level in center field. Although Maddox went hitless against the A's, he did manage to reach on an error. The fleet footed Maddox, who had stolen as many as twenty bases in a part time role with Texas, was restricted by Bill Virdon's tendency to forego the use of the stolen base as a strategic weapon. Despite being the fastest member of the starting lineup, Maddox did not join veterans Roy White and Bobby Murcer as the only Yankees to reach double-digits in steals in 1974. Players of White and Murcer's status were much more willing to use their own initiative rather than waiting for a steal sign from the bench, but at this late point in the season Maddox had been restricted to only six steal attempts. The game with the A's was close, and with the score 1-0 in favor of the Yankees Maddox attempted a relatively rare steal of second base. Injured on the slide, the rising star was removed from the game and would miss the next four games.

Walter Williams, who replaced Maddox, hit a single in his lone trip to the plate on that day. This would not have been noteworthy if not for the fact that Williams had previously been 0-for-July. And 0-for-June. And 0-for-May. In fact, that single by Walt Williams was his first hit in three months. The hard working outfielder had gone 0-29 during that stretch, seeing his batting average drop to .059. It is difficult for any hitter to come to the plate only twenty-nine times over a three month period and remain sharp with the bat, and Williams was certainly no exception. He started only two games during that stretch, and both of those had come in April. Even with Maddox sidelined he would get but one start in the field. The man who feared a loss of playing time upon his acquisition by the Yankees was in fact buried very deeply on the Yankee bench. Yet, he performed a very important role. Winning teams need players who can fill a variety of roles with some degree of competency. These players need the temperament and work ethic to accept this unheralded assignment and be ready to play when the time came. In the case of Walt Williams in 1974 this meant stepping in at a moment's notice to pinch hit, pinch run, enter a game as a defensive replacement, and fill in with the occasional start. It is a necessary but thankless role. It was not a role that pleased Williams, who told one reporter "I would give half my salary to return to Cleveland." Yet the effervescent Williams remained outwardly cheerful and he was a source of fun and positive energy in the clubhouse.

After a single, rare start during the brief absence of Maddox from the lineup, Williams would go only 2-15 over the remainder of the year, raising his batting average to a paltry .113. The .116 average of his predecessor, Ron Swoboda, had resulted in Swoboda's release. Still, the Yankees realized the unique value that Williams offered and retained him for the 1975 season. When a plethora of injuries to outfielders resulted in a much greater opportunity to appear in the lineup, Williams rebounded with a .281 batting average in what would be his final major league season.

Keystone

One of the primary concerns of Yankee management entering the 1974 campaign was the quality of their middle infielders. Jim Mason's opening day start at shortstop was no guarantee that the job would remain his throughout the season. Just twenty-three and possessing a reputation for a strong glove offset by a weak bat, the newcomer overcame a slow start to show enough offensive production that he was able to retain his hold on the position throughout the season, including a game against his former Texas teammates in which he hit four doubles. In fact, a strong finish left Mason with a very respectable .250 batting average, highlighted by an impressive .284 average against right-handed pitching. At a time in which premium shortstops were in very short supply, Mason held his own against his peers in the league. His 144 games started was the most of any Yankee at the shortstop position since Tony Kubek started 145 times thirteen years earlier. He may not have been the best in the game, but Jim Mason was able to alleviate some of the concerns about the shortstop role. Second base had been a completely different matter, but all of that was about to change.

To some baseball fans Sandy Alomar's biggest contribution to the sport was siring two superstars, sons Sandy Jr. and Roberto. But Sandy's legacy extends well beyond fatherhood. The elder Alomar had his own career which spanned fifteen major league seasons with five different clubs. His career statistics are underwhelming. A player known for durability, versatility, and speed, the only things he ever led a league in were games played, plate appearances, and at bats, and those accomplishments occurred while he was in the employ of the California

Angels during a period when the club's roster was thin at best. In contrast with his more powerful offspring, he managed only thirteen home runs in over five thousand plate appearances. He arrived in the major leagues in 1964 at the age of twenty and became the Milwaukee Braves starting shortstop during a late-season call up. Sandy was unable to stick in a crowded Braves infield and he found himself splitting time between the Braves and AAA before being traded to Houston along with Braves legend Eddie Mathews after the 1966 season. Alomar's stay with the Astros was short, as he was quickly dispatched to the Mets a few weeks later without ever wearing an Astros uniform. Alomar stuck with the Mets to start the 1967 season as a pinch runner and utility infielder, going 0-for-New York with no hits in twenty-two plate appearances. That slow start, coupled with an .091 batting average in forty-four at bats with Atlanta in 1966, suggested that Alomar was not yet capable of hitting at the big league level. His record upon returning to AAA indicated that he couldn't hit at that level either, and he found himself on the move again, this time as a throw-in in a late season trade with the Chicago White Sox. This proved to be something of a stroke of luck for Alomar. The White Sox had a very weak roster and a hole at second base. Alomar began the 1968 season on the bench again, but by July he was playing every day over an extended period for the first time in his career. Less than a year later he was sent to the Angels, were he continued to hold the job as everyday second baseman. Alomar would own that job until well into the 1973 season, making the All-Star team in 1970. Alomar's run as the Angels second baseman came to an end in September of 1973, when a broken leg prematurely ended his season and opened up the door for Billy Parker to take his spot. When the season ended the Angels acquired Denny Doyle, an ominous sign that Alomar's time as the team's second baseman might be coming to a conclusion. Parker was drafted by the Yankees the following winter, and Alomar's name was also rumored to be on the list of middle infielders coveted by the New Yorkers. The Yankees chose not to conclude a deal for Alomar until seeing evidence that he had fully healed from the broken leg that he had suffered the previous September. Instead of following Billy Parker to New York, Sandy Alomar opened the 1974 season as an unhappy backup to Doyle. Alomar would spend the first three months on the bench, leaving only occasionally to pinch hit, pinch run, or fill in one of the infield spots. He was thirty, hitting .220, and had only a single run batted in to show for over fifty at bats. It was not unreasonable to conclude that Sandy Alomar's days as a big league player were numbered.

Meanwhile in Flushing Meadows, the Yankees had still not found a satisfactory answer to their lingering second base question. By this point the club had tried Gene Michael, Horace Clarke, Fernando Gonzalez, and Fred Stanley at second base, and none of them provided even the minimal amount of production required to end the quest for a permanent solution. At the beginning of July Michael and Gonzalez were splitting time at the position, but the Yankees were still not satisfied and decided it was time to try yet another move. On July 8 the Yankees purchased Sandy Alomar from the Angels.

There was no reason to expect that this latest move would result in anything but one more entrant to the revolving door at second base in the Yankee lineup. A day after joining the Yankees Alomar debuted in the same role he had left behind in California, pinch running in his first appearance in pinstripes. He moved into the starting role the next day. After a week he was hitting just .143, though he had doubled his RBI output with the Angels by knocking in two runs. Still, with no remaining competition for the starting spot, Sandy Alomar would start at second base for forty-nine of the next fifty games.

The choice of Alomar as the de facto solution to the Yankee second base conundrum is particularly interesting in light of the fact that this was the same Yankee club that was so eager to put the Horace Clarke Era behind them. Though Clarke was four years older, the two men were remarkably similar in many ways. Both were switch hitters, both counted on speed to offset relative weaknesses in their offensive ability, and both were durable and versatile players. Clarke was slightly better offensively, while Alomar posted slightly higher stolen base totals. The main difference between the two was their defensive ability. Though not a defensive star, Alomar was arguably at least one or two notches above Clarke with the glove, and it was that asset that helped make Alomar a fixture at second base for the remainder of the 1974 season. Better still, Alomar seemed to have a knack at doing the little things, contributing to the offense in ways that Clarke had not done. A timely hit, a walk, moving a runner over – these were all parts of Alomar's game, and it was no coincidence that his ascension to the Yankee keystone position provided a spark to the offense and the defense that helped light the Yankees' pennant dreams. The Yankees were a different club with Sandy Alomar at second base.

Alomar's arrival came not a moment too soon. The Yankees took the field on July 4 having lost nine out of their last ten games, culminating in a season-worst seven game losing streak. The Yankees rebounded by winning nine out of ten, including a six game winning streak that began on July 8, coinciding with the arrival of Alomar. The streak that began on that night, their longest of the season to that point, featured the reawakening of the Yankee offense as the club outscored their opponents 46-18 during the streak. As the offense was starting to heat up, the starting rotation was keeping them in almost every game. The bullpen was also coming through, though Virdon's hands-off style limited save opportunities. Sparky Lyle, who had saved sixty-two games in the last two seasons under Ralph Houk, went the entire month of June without a save while the entire pitching staff only recorded two during that time. Still, Virdon's approach seemed to be having a positive impact and the though the Yankees were still stuck in last place they were now playing their best baseball of the season.

July 13, 1974	W	L	PCT	GB
Baltimore Orioles	47	39	.547	-
Cleveland Indians	46	39	.541	0.5
Boston Red Sox	47	40	.540	0.5
Milwaukee Brewers	44	42	.512	3
Detroit Tigers	44	43	.506	3.5
New York Yankees	44	43	.506	3.5

Breakout Game

If the sudden change in fortune seemed too good to be true, the Yankees ran smack into a dose of reality on July 10. Rudy May, whose presence had revived the Yankee pitching staff, jammed his ankle fielding a bunt on the artificial turf in Kansas City. The injury cost him three weeks on the disabled list. Sam McDowell was activated from that same list to take May's place, but an eight walk performance in the first start after his return did little to enhance confidence in the veteran. Dave Pagan posted his only win of the season with a complete game victory the day before May's injury, but then failed to get past the fifth inning in his next three starts. The depleted Yankee pitching staff was unable to absorb the loss of a key pitcher, and May's loss was having a domino effect across the staff. With McDowell and Pagan unable to compensate for May's absence, the entire pitching staff felt the strain and the club ended the month of July with a five game losing streak. The Yankees outlook had improved with the arrival of Rudy May and Sandy Alomar and they had managed to keep their record above the .500 mark, but the club was still at the bottom of the standings and was running out of time to make an impact on the eastern division standings.

On a much more positive note, Doc Medich continued to solidify his place among the league's top young pitchers. The man who scared off so many potential major league employers because of his long term commitment to medical school had earned his eleventh victory by the midpoint of the season and was already closing in on the fourteen wins he secured during his successful debut season a year before.

Yankee Resurrection

On July 20 the Yankees were still at the bottom of the standings and a game under the .500 mark as they hosted the Kansas City Royals for a matinee at Shea Stadium. On the mound for the Royals was Steve Busby, whose successful rookie season matched that which Medich had enjoyed a year earlier. The Royals featured a solid lineup that would evolve to dominate the western division in the second half of the 1970s.

Busby found a rude reception that afternoon and was in the showers midway through the second inning on the short side of a 4-0 score. Medich, on the other hand, was cruising through the Royals lineup. The only blemish occurred in the third inning when future Hall of Famer George Brett, a rising star still establishing his reputation and hitting eighth in the batting order, hit a fly ball to left center field. Blinded by the sun and perhaps victimized by a slight lack of communication, Roy White and Elliott Maddox let the ball fall between them. There is no such thing as a "team error" in baseball, and balls lost in the sun are generally therefore scored as hits. The exception tends to be when the play would represent the first hit of the day, as was the case on this day. Elliott Maddox, being nearest to the ball, was therefore charged with an error. For the next five innings it appeared to be a critical scoring decision.

The "error" by Maddox and walks to Cookie Rojas and John Mayberry were the only baserunners for the Royals through the first eight innings. Medich was just three outs away from becoming the first Yankee to pitch a no hitter since Don Larsen's perfect game in the 1956 World Series. The lineup appeared to fall in Medich's favor, with number nine hitter catcher Fran Healy, light hitting Freddie Patek, and slumping Vada Pinson due up in the ninth for the Royals. Medich's shot at immortality ended when Healy lined a clean single to center. Pinch hitter Richie Scheinblum followed with a double. A wild pitch and a groundout resulted in two runs – Medich had lost the no hitter and a shutout, but held on to win the game 6-2. Though the performance went into the books as "just another" two hitter, it was one more indication that this Yankee team had potential, perhaps as yet not fully tapped, to achieve great things.

Bystander?

Albert "Sparky" Lyle was something of a late bloomer. Although the pitcher would one day earn a place in history as one of the pioneer "closers" who came into games in the late innings to protect a lead, often interrupting an otherwise effective pitching performance by the starter, his early record showed few hints of future stardom. As a pioneer in the art of relief pitching, Lyle found himself in the relief role via a similar route taken by most relief pitchers of his day – by beginning as a starter. Signed in 1964 at the age of nineteen by the Baltimore Orioles, Lyle was sent to the lowest depths of the Oriole minor league system where he started ten of the thirteen games that he pitched at that level. Lyle caught the attention of the Boston Red Sox, who drafted the youngster prior to the 1965 season. From that point forward the young southpaw was used almost exclusively in relief. He made the last start of his career on the last day of the Pittsfield Red Sox 1965 season. Manager Eddie Popowski asked for a volunteer to start the game and Lyle enthusiastically raised his hand. Lyle responded by pitching a one hit complete game shutout, with his near perfect game spoiled only by a bunt single by speedy former major leaguer Howie Bedell. By this time Lyle's trademark slider, a pitch that he had taught himself and perfected by spending hours throwing against a brick wall, began to show promise to the point of being almost unhittable at the AAA level. The Red Sox recognized Lyle's progression and rewarded the reliever with a promotion to the Red Sox midway through their Impossible Dream season in 1967, during which the club rose from a ninth place finish the year before to winning the American League championship in dramatic fashion on the last weekend of the season. Pitching under the pressure of a pennant race that had drawn national attention, Lyle performed brilliantly before being shut down with a sore arm just prior to the World Series. Lyle quietly filled the role as the number one Red Sox relief pitcher from 1968-1971. Lyle's performance was largely under the radar of most of the baseball world given the fact that the Red Sox were not postseason contenders during the remainder of Lyle's time with the club and the fact that Lyle began his career during a time when relief pitchers did not accumulate the huge save totals that their successors would later enjoy. Ironically, it was Lyle himself who would go a long way toward changing that.

By 1971 the Red Sox had accumulated a plethora of left handed pitching. Lyle shared relief duties with lefties Bill Lee and Ken Brett, while lefty rookies Rogelio Moret and John Curtis were already auditioning for future roles with the big club. With Lyle checking in as the elder statesman of the group at age twenty-seven, he was a logical candidate to use as trade bait. The Sox desperately needed a first baseman, to the point where they considered moving star outfielder Carl Yastrzemski to first base. The Yankees had long tried to negotiate a deal for Lyle as they saw the lefty as an excellent counterbalance to a bullpen dominated by right handers. With veteran Felipe Alou and the newly-acquired Rich McKinney and Hal Lanier available as right handed bats at the corner infield positions, first baseman Danny Cater was available as trade bait. And so it was that a trade of Lyle for Cater and rookie infielder Mario Guerrero was consummated at the end of spring training in 1972. Lyle was a very welcomed addition to an anemic Yankee bullpen – his sixteen saves in 1971 was four more than *total* number of saves earned by the entire Yankee pitching staff. While both teams welcomed the deal, it was anything but a blockbuster. In exchange for a reliable though largely unremarkable relief pitcher the Yankees had sent the Red Sox a reliable though largely unremarkable infielder. Cater was five years older than Lyle, and while he had batted .301 and .276 in two seasons with the Yankees and was well recognized as an excellent line drive hitter, he had displayed little power. It would not be long before that narrative completely changed. Cater struggled with the Red Sox while Lyle flourished with his new club, earning a whopping thirty-five saves. The newly minted superstar finished third in the voting for Most Valuable Player (in an odd contrast, he finished seventh in the Cy Young Award voting). In prior times relief pitchers were generally called in to save games only when starters or other relief pitchers found themselves in trouble, hence the nickname "fireman" for the role. Yankee Manager Ralph Houk used Lyle differently, bringing Lyle in to preempt trouble. It was a technique that Houk had used with great success as far back as his first season as field general in 1961, when Luis Arroyo saved twenty-nine games, including thirteen games in which ace Whitey Ford was the winning pitcher. This innovation garnered lingering criticism from Yankee haters who derided Arroyo's role and claimed that it artificially inflated Whitey Ford's win totals, caustically suggesting that Ford should have to share his Cy Young Award with his reliever. The strange criticism that this new tactic was somehow enabling starting pitchers to be more successful bothered Houk little, but the scarcity of top-notch relief specialists forced him to curtail the practice until the emergence of Jack Aker and Lindy McDaniel nine years later. That duo saved forty-five games between them in 1970, a significant factor in the team's surprising second place finish. Evidence of Houk's use of Lyle can be found in one particularly telling statistic – years before the term closer was invented,

Lyle was the final pitcher in fifty-six of the fifty-nine games he appeared in during the 1972 season.

In addition to winning the hearts of Yankee fans, Lyle became one of the most popular players in the Yankee clubhouse. Lyle's crazy antics and legendary pranks made him a centerpiece of clubhouse life. His free spirited attitude did not distract him from proving that his 1972 performance was no fluke, as he posted a very impressive save total of twenty-seven in 1973. Lyle's closer role under Houk was clear, but by 1974 Houk was gone and Lyle would become one of the many examples of the very stark differences between Ralph Houk and Bill Virdon.

The Pittsburgh Pirate ball club that Bill Virdon managed was called the Pittsburgh Lumber Company, a nickname that was attached to the club in the early 1970s but had its origins in the prior decade when Virdon was still a fixture in the Pirate outfield. This was a period in which the Pirate lineup was stacked from top to bottom with some of the best hitters in the National League. Even Pirate pitchers developed a reputation for swinging dangerous bats. With a lineup populated by sluggers, it is a perfectly reasonable strategy to let hitters swing the bat and wait for a big inning. In Virdon's first year as Pirate skipper his club led the league in hitting by fourteen points but also came close to leading the league in men left on base. Virdon's station-to-station approach left the Pirates last in the league in stolen base attempts and last in sacrifice bunts. Like Lyle, Pittsburgh's ace reliever Dave Giusti saw a significant drop in save opportunities under new manager Virdon. Virdon's second and final year with the Pirates produced a similar resistance to playing small ball, earning

Virdon the reputation as a hands-off manager with a minimalist approach to in-game offensive decisions. This reputation followed him to New York, where the Yankee lineup lacked the power and depth of Virdon's Pirates and where big innings were preciously few and far between.

Bill Virdon did deliver on a primary expectation of George Steinbrenner and Gabe Paul – to break up the status quo and whip the Yankees into a disciplined team that was strong in the fundamental aspects of the game. In this aspect he was the right man in the right role at the right time for the Yankees. Still, Virdon was clearly not the prototypical George Steinbrenner manager. George Steinbrenner expected his managers to be highly visible, energetic, hands-on cheerleaders for the ball club. The owner's vision of the perfect manger is one whose cunning tactics reflect the Boss's ingenuity in hiring him, and one who rallies his troops to run through walls in order to bring home a win for the team. Ralph Houk definitely did not fit that pattern, and Bill Virdon was even farther from the Steinbrenner ideal than Houk. Decades before over-managing would become a frequent criticism (and sometimes compliment) for managers, Virdon could safely be classified as one of the least influential in-game skippers in the business. Once the season began, Virdon's laisse-fare attitude did not go unnoticed by either his players or his boss. Virdon was a delegator, a trait that was anathema to a boss whose hands-on style was legendary. Virdon drove Steinbrenner crazy by sending third base coach Dick Howser out to most pregame umpire meetings and pitching coach Whitey Ford out to the mound to make pitching changes. While this was something of an exception among his managerial peers, it was not unheard of. In the clubhouse Virdon had become the subject of rumblings for his reluctance to employ standard small ball tactics during the games, to the point that some veteran players created their own signs for bunting, stealing bases, and executing the hit-and-run play. Such grumbling does not appear to be justified and may have been more of a reflection of Virdon's unpopularity compared to the departed Houk and a reflection of his prior reputation as a hands-off skipper. The 1974 Yankees logged only two less base stealing attempts than their 1973 counterparts and almost doubled their predecessor's successful sacrifice attempts. While some of these statistics might have been a result of players calling their own plays, the numbers indicate that Virdon's in-game play calling was not very different from his predecessor. In terms of pitching changes, Virdon's 1974 team logged six more complete games than Houk's 1973 squad, a number no doubt influenced by the fact that the team also won more games than their predecessors. Still, as with most ball clubs the starters complained that they were lifted too early and the relievers complained that Virdon stayed with the starters too long. Notwithstanding all of the complaining, virtually all statistical evidence shows that the managerial tendencies between Ralph Houk and Bill Virdon were more similar that the players might like to admit.

Still, there were two very noteworthy differences between Houk and Virdon's managerial styles. First was Houk's affinity for platooning, a tactic pioneered by Houk's mentor Casey Stengel. Yankee slugger Ron Blomberg best illustrates Houk's attitude toward the platoon system. Despite having a career best season in 1973, the lefty hitter was permitted only seventeen at bats against left handed pitching. Under Virdon, Blomberg was subjected to occasional platooning but saw significantly more left handed pitching, rewarding the manager's confidence by hitting a respectable .276 against southpaws. Virdon publicly acknowledged his belief that Blomberg belonged in the lineup every day. Far more striking was Virdon's use of the bullpen, as the number of saves plummeted in his first year as skipper and would fall even further in his second. Part of the decline was due to changes in the save rule which limited the number of situations in which a save could be earned to reduce scenarios in which relievers could pick up saves in games in which the score was not close. The Yankees were generally not a team that blew the opposition away, so the majority of Lyle's saves under Houk would still be saves under the new rule. The main difference was that Houk would call on Lyle pretty much any time after the sixth inning if the Yankees had a lead of three runs or less, something Virdon was far less likely to do. Virdon's departure from leveraging Sparky Lyle as the team's closer was clearly noted by the players and would later become the subject of a feeding frenzy of second guessing.

Whatever the players thought of Virdon's managerial tendencies, the new manager had kept the club within striking distance of the top of the division despite being in last place as the club passed the midseason point in July. At this point the club went through a series of tantalizing hot streaks followed by frustrating losing streaks. By August 2 the team was still mired in last place, three games under the .500 mark and now six and half games out of the top spot. Worse still, the division-leading Red Sox were starting to show signs of pulling ahead of the pack, with the surprising Cleveland Indians, their roster packed with former Yankees, exceeding expectations and continuing to hint at a possible run for the title. Despite all of the player moves and the "win at all costs" attitude of Gabe

Bystander?

Paul and George Steinbrenner, Yankee fans could be forgiven for resigning themselves to another poor finish in the standings. Time was running out on the 1974 season.

August 2, 1974	W	L	PCT	GB
Boston Red Sox	57	47	.548	-
Cleveland Indians	54	49	.524	2.5
Baltimore Orioles	52	52	.500	5
Detroit Tigers	51	53	.490	6
Milwaukee Brewers	51	54	.486	6.5
New York Yankees	51	54	.486	6.5

On Fire

On August 19 Sudden Sam McDowell started for the New York Yankees for the last time. The former star whose arrival a year before had helped cement the new Yankee management team's commitment to success had exhausted the club's patience by failing to get past the second inning and losing his sixth game in seven decisions. With the exception of a September relief appearance, McDowell was finished with the Yankees. McDowell was about to become part of an illustration of a peculiar exercise in baseball math – addition by subtraction. In this case, the subtraction of a poor performing veteran paved the way for the addition of a high achieving newcomer.

Larry Gura would not exactly fit Central Casting's image of an athlete whose arrival would fuel their team's turnaround. By the time he was traded to the Yankees from Texas in May in exchange for Duke Sims, the twenty-six year-old had already logged parts of four undistinguished major league seasons. After a successful college career with the legendary Arizona State University baseball team, Gura was chosen by the Chicago Cubs as their second pick in the 1969 draft. After performing well in two partial seasons in the Cubs' minor league system, Gura was promoted to the big club in mid-1970, joining a team that was in the thick of a pennant race. The young southpaw performed admirably, but soon found himself ensconced in veteran manager Leo Durocher's very, very crowded doghouse. The abrasive Durocher, notoriously unpopular with both his own players and his opponents, had a long history of verbally abusing young players. Gura's offense was that the pitcher, who was the personification of the "craft lefty," lacked aggressiveness and did not challenge hitters. Thus labeled, Gura found himself shuttling between the minor leagues and the back bench of Durocher's bullpen for the manager's last two years with the club. Gura fared little better under new manager Whitey Lockman in 1973 and found himself wearing the uniform of the Texas Rangers in the spring of 1974. It was at that point that Gura's luck with managers went from bad to worse. Ranger manager Billy Martin was in many ways cut from the same cloth as the elder Durocher, and Martin took an immediate dislike to Gura. Martin's disdain for Gura was allegedly fueled even further by Gura's fondness for tennis, an activity in which he engaged during spring training. While activities like golf were seen as quite acceptable spring training distractions for ballplayers throughout Martin's days in baseball, the very opinionated manager saw tennis as a game unbecoming of "real men." Gura had no future on Billy Martin's club. Demoted to the minor leagues once again, even the trade to the Yankees was initially not enough to elevate him to the majors. Gura accepted his relegation to the minor leagues for the fifth year in a row and addressed it by turning in one of the best performances of his professional career. Despite Gura's minor league success it was Dave Pagan who was initially chosen to replace Mel Stottlemyre and to fill in for Rudy May during his time on the disabled list. A series of poor starts by Pagan, coupled with McDowell's implosion, finally paved the way for Gura to be recalled for what would become a ten year run as an effective major league pitcher.

The loss by McDowell on August 19 had once again dropped the Yankees below the .500 mark. The team was now seven games out of first place with only forty-one games left in the season. As the team marked the one-year anniversary of the start of the 1973 team's self-destructive slide to fourth place, there was absolutely no reason for Yankee fans to feel energized or optimistic about the current team's chances.

Regardless of what the fans might think, the attitude in the Yankee clubhouse was quite different than it had been a year before. Rather than fading under the pressure of the club's poor performance, this version of the Yankees was as loose as can be. With the strains of "Band on the Run" blasting in the clubhouse and on the field, the team flourished in their role of written-off underdogs.

The day after McDowell's loss a Pat Dobson complete game victory over the Twins triggered a five game winning streak, capped off by Gura's debut four days later when the newcomer defeated the legendary Nolan Ryan with a masterful 2-1 complete game performance. Each game of the streak featured a different player delivering a clutch hitting performance in support of outstanding starting pitching. The only blemish on the pitcher's mound occurred when Rudy May was again sidelined by an injury. When healthy, May had been sensational since joining New York. The highlight of his season came after his return from the disabled list in early August. May delivered three consecutive complete game victories, spreading thirteen hits across twenty-seven innings without giving up a single earned run. May's run of success ended when he was forced to leave his next two starts early. Even this setback failed to derail the Yankees as relievers Mike Wallace and Dick Tidrow stepped up to nail down victories.

A single loss was followed by a six game winning streak that landed the Yankees a single game out of first place by Labor Day. Pat Dobson was in the process of turning around what had previously been a disappointing season that had left the veteran pitcher with a 10-14 record in mid-August. Dobson would go on to chalk up nine victories in his final ten decisions of the year, barely missing his second twenty win season. Thurman Munson had finally shaken his season-long slump, adding twenty points to his batting average in the month of August.

A season that had seemed to be a lost cause just two weeks earlier was suddenly seen in a whole new light. The pennant race that Yankee fans had dreamed of since 1964 was now looking like a reality. The Yankees were now the hottest team in the American League east and it was now quite conceivable that an improbable run to the postseason had begun.

September 2, 1974	W	L	PCT	GB
Boston Red Sox	72	62	.537	-
New York Yankees	71	63	.530	1
Baltimore Orioles	69	65	.515	3
Cleveland Indians	65	66	.496	5.5
Milwaukee Brewers	65	71	.478	8
Detroit Tigers	62	71	.466	9.5

Penalty Box

The rules governing contributions to political campaigns have a long history of being very complicated and a long history of being ignored or clandestinely bypassed. In this landscape it was not extremely unusual for George Steinbrenner and his American Shipbuilding Company to become embroiled in controversy involving illegal contributions to the 1972 campaign to re-elect President Richard M. Nixon. Steinbrenner was accused of trying to cover up a $25,000 campaign contribution by passing funds through employees of his shipbuilding company. The attempt to hide the illegal donations allegedly continued while an investigation into the financing of the campaign was launched. Steinbrenner eventually reversed course and agreed to cooperate with authorities. Nixon resigned from office on August 9, 1974, and two weeks later George Steinbrenner entered a guilty plea, admitting to the contributions and to the cover up attempt. In addition to a charge of making an illegal campaign contribution, Steinbrenner's guilty pleas covered his lies to authorities, resulting in a felony obstruction of justice conviction and a $15,000 fine. On September 6 Major League Baseball Commissioner Bowie Kuhn, using his authority to protect the "best interests of baseball," suspended Steinbrenner from direct action with the ball club that he owned. The suspension was temporary, initially covering a thirty day period while Kuhn continued his review of the case. Just over two months later Kuhn completed his review and sentenced the Yankee owner to a two year suspension from the role of general partner.

As the Band on the Run prepared to meet the unexpected opportunity to conduct a stretch run toward a divisional title, they could now rest assured that they would do so without obvious hands-on meddling by their owner.

Reinforcements

It is a common practice in most organized sports to restrict teams from materially changing their rosters late in the season, with the theory that teams contending for a championship should do so with the players who put them into contention while not being unfairly assisted by other teams looking to clear their roster. With this in mind, Major League Baseball established roster restrictions that became progressively tighter as the season progressed. Under these rules, teams could not make player moves with another club after mid-June without the implicit approval, or waiver, of clubs below them in the standings. Two additional rules took effect on September 1. As of that day, only players who were on the twenty-five man active roster (with the exception of players on the disabled list) were eligible for postseason play. This meant that anyone acquired or brought up from the minor leagues after that date was ineligible for any postseason action. The second rule allowed teams to expand their active rosters from twenty-five to forty players for the remainder of the season. This gave teams the opportunity to promote prospects from the minor leagues and evaluate them in a big league setting as they prepared for the next season, while giving fans a taste of the future. Doc Medich, Ron Blomberg, Graig Nettles, Lou Piniella, Bobby Murcer, Roy White, and Thurman Munson all enjoyed September previews early in their careers. The roster expansion also allowed teams to supplement their rosters with specialists to fill important needs like pinch runners, defensive replacements, and additional pitching. These minor leaguers, along with any player acquired from outside of the organization after September 1, were available to assist their clubs in their final drive for a title but would have to watch postseason games on television like any other fan. Still, the addition of a few extra weapons in their arsenal was a priority for virtually every contending team, and the 1974 Yankees were no exception.

August had been a relatively quiet month for player moves as teams began to position themselves for the stretch run. Cleveland's August 17 acquisition of designated hitter Rico Carty, who had spent most of the 1974 season in the Mexican League, was the last major acquisition prior to the roster freeze. The veteran Carty was a former batting champion who even in his prime was a major liability in the field, making him an ideal designated hitter candidate. Carty was no stranger to the role of late-season addition, having played that role the previous September as Oakland sought to lock up the American League west title. The thirty-four year-old Carty rewarded the Indians with a .363 batting average over the remainder of the season.

The close race in the A.L. East had teams burning the phone lines trying to round out their rosters. Boston struck first in September, netting veteran catcher Tim McCarver to boost their bench. A week later the Sox struck again with the acquisition of Deron Johnson from the fading Milwaukee Brewers. The Orioles acquired talented veterans Bob Oliver and Jim Northrup, while the Indians added Frank Robinson to their lineup.

Despite the avowed commitment to leave no stone unturned and pay any reasonable price in the quest for talent, the Yankees were unusually quiet after the acquisition of Sandy Alomar in early July. The club finally broke through and completed a September 9 purchase of Alex Johnson from their frequent partners, the Texas Rangers. Although it was past the postseason roster lockdown, the Yankees saw this as a low risk path to improving their right handed designated hitter role.

At first glance, Texas's divestment of a talented player like Johnson for so little in return while they were embroiled in their own stretch drive might seem a little strange. The Rangers had just completed a three game sweep of division-leading Oakland and had climbed to within five and a half games of the Athletics with three more games against the first place club scheduled for a few days later. One might think that the Rangers might feel the need to keep their roster loaded so that every possible contingency was addressed as the team faced their own do-or-die contests in search of their first championship. Johnson had posted a .291 batting average with the Rangers, and as recently as mid-August he was a regular part of the starting lineup. Johnson's playing time had decreased significantly, and had not appeared in a single game for Texas in the month of September. His primary replacement was Joe Lovitto, a more capable defender in the outfield but a .216 lifetime hitter. All Texas manager Billy Martin would say about the divestment of Johnson was that he thought "Alex would be happier somewhere else."

Alex Johnson ranks among the greatest enigmas in the history of baseball, and Billy Martin's vague parting comment about Johnson surprised no one in the baseball world. Alex Johnson made his big league debut ten years earlier with the Philadelphia Phillies after hitting over .300 at every level of the minor leagues. He immediately displayed the clear talent with the bat and the bizarre personality that would define him for the remainder of his baseball career. It was during Johnson's time with the Phillies that he garnered his first bevy of criticism for not consistently giving his best effort. His relationship with his teammates was also unusual. Some called him "misunderstood," although it is easy to see how a man who had trouble remembering the names of his fellow players, opting instead to address all of his teammates as simply "Dickhead", could be looked at a little oddly by those same teammates. Johnson's reputation as a problem player grew, and over a thirteen year major league career he would play for eight different teams, never surviving more than two seasons at any stop and never returning to a club that had previously dealt him away. Despite the baggage that he carried, his credentials as an elite hitter were so well established that his services were in regular demand by teams who believed they could succeed in addressing his personality quirks. By 1970 none of Johnson's three previous employers had solved the Alex Johnson puzzle but the California Angels decided to take up the challenge. Johnson rewarded their confidence in him by capturing the American League batting title. Even that achievement was not enough to change the trajectory of his career. A year later he was the focal point of an implosion in the Angels clubhouse as the outfielder was admonished, fined, and suspended for infractions and accusations ranging from failure to hustle to fighting with his teammates. At one point Johnson claimed that teammate Chico Ruiz, who at one time was Johnson's best and perhaps only friend on the team, had threatened him with a gun. Though there were no witnesses and the allegation was never proved, Johnson's teammates sided with Ruiz. The Angels eventually suspended Johnson for the maximum thirty days, and Commissioner Bowie Kuhn stepped in and extended the suspension for the remainder of the season. The news of Johnson's suspension was received with an ovation in the Angel clubhouse. In their defense of Johnson, the Major League Baseball Players

Association claimed, with some validity, that Johnson was suffering from psychiatric issues and should thus not be punished with suspension but given the same support as any other injured or sick player. Their appeal was denied. Johnson would remain on the suspended list for the entire second half of the 1971 season. A postseason trade to Cleveland enabled Johnson to resume his career. After a single season in Cleveland, the former batting champion was dealt to Texas, where he enjoyed a comeback that saw him hit .287 in 1973 and .291 in 1974 before the Rangers shipped him and his .291 career batting average to the Yankees for their September stretch run.

While little help was available from outside of the organization, the Yankees were able to tap into their minor league system for some additional roster assistance. Left handed relief specialist Tippy Martinez filled in for an ailing Lyle in late August and provided additional bullpen depth in September. Highly rated prospect Otto Velez saw sporadic playing time in the latter weeks of the season, although his playing time would be reduced by the arrival of the more seasoned Alex Johnson. The club also added twenty-one year-old outfielder Larry Murray as a pinch running specialist. Murray was one of the fastest players in organized baseball, with sixty-two stolen bases to his credit during his time in Ft. Lauderdale in 1974. This statistic is all the more amazing considering that the youngster hit only .207, although he was incredibly prolific at drawing walks. Murray's inability to hit professional pitching would prove to be the Achilles heel that robbed him of a successful major league career, but his foot speed made him a highly anticipated addition to the Yankee roster.

Reinforcements

The other newcomer of note was utility infielder Fred Stanley. Stanley, who had already played in parts of five prior major league seasons, had held the starting second base role for a week in June as part of the revolving door at that position prior to the arrival of Sandy Alomar. In fact, it was Alomar's arrival that resulted in Stanley's demotion back to the minor leagues. Stanley would play eleven games in September and bat only eight times, but his presence on the bench gave manager Virdon much needed flexibility at second base and shortstop late in games down the stretch.

One player that the Yankees would not be able to count on as the season wore down was pitcher Sam McDowell. Unable to pitch effectively and frustrated by being passed over for stretch drive starts in favor of lefties Larry Gura and Mike Wallace, McDowell jumped the club after pitching his last game in pinstripes on September 8. McDowell would be released by the Yankees the following January, and after a brief comeback with Pittsburgh in 1975 he would hang up his spikes. Sam McDowell later recovered from his alcohol addiction and would go on to have a tremendous impact as an alcohol counselor. McDowell's final role with organized baseball was as a frequent guest in team clubhouses where his story of addiction and recovery touched many players with similar afflictions.

As a footnote to the activity surrounding the Yankee roster, it is important to note two players who had been with the club since the beginning of the season but who saw their scarce playing time further dwindle with the influx of new arrivals. Bill Sudakis had begun the season as a frequent first baseman and designated hitter, but the installation of Chris Chambliss as the everyday first baseman and the emergence of Elliot Maddox and Lou Piniella had landed Sudakis on the bench. Outside of a start in the second game of a September 7 double header Sudakis had warmed the bench through the final month of the season. The acquisition of Johnson had further diminished the relevance of Sudakis, as Johnson became Virdon's first option when a right handed designated hitter or pinch hitter was required.

Like Sudakis, backup catcher Rick Dempsey had found his meager playing time reduced even further in the final month of the season as he served as understudy to Thurman Munson. Like former manager Ralph Houk, Dempsey had learned the frustration of spending the majority of the season sitting on the bench behind a star catcher. In the case of backing up Munson, the assignment was even more frustrating because no matter how beat up the catcher was there was no way to pry him from the catcher's box unless he was completely incapable of playing. The hand injury that Munson suffered at the end of spring training continued to plague him all season long, but the stubborn catcher insisted on playing through the pain. Dempsey replaced the injured Munson by starting seventeen games behind the plate over a three week period in late spring, but beyond that was limited to only seven starts the entire rest of the season. Known primarily as a defensive specialist with a questionable bat, the Yankees did not have enough confidence in Dempsey to sacrifice Munson's bat in the lineup during the stretch drive. Like Sudakis, Dempsey was limited to a single start in September after starting only two games in August, with his only other appearances coming when Virdon rested Munson late in two blowout games. Baseball players are proud competitors, and despite the wave of success enjoyed by the Yankees and the joy and exhilaration of a pennant race, both Sudakis and Dempsey felt their frustration grow as they watched their teammates from the dugout and the bullpen. That growing frustration would one day have serious consequences for the Yankees.

Pennant Race

The Yankees remained red hot as the month of September progressed. As is the story with most winning teams, each winning game featured a new hero. The 1974 Yankee roster featured no superstars – when the final votes for the league's Most Valuable Player Award were tallied only, Elliot Maddox would appear in the top ten with an eighth place finish. Not a single Yankee pitcher would earn a point in the Cy Young Award voting. Yet the team was achieving an outcome unseen in recent years – the performance of the team as a whole transcended the sum of individual performances.

In the midst of the balanced offensive attack pieced together by Gabe Paul there were noteworthy performances. The aforementioned Maddox continued his breakout season into September. Maddox, whose previous high batting average in four major league seasons was .252, saw his average climb above the .300 mark with a three hit performance on June 1. It stayed above that level for the rest of the season. Another consistently bright offensive light was provided by the veteran Lou Piniella. Piniella had begun the season without a clearly defined role, starting only two of the team's first nine games of the season. Unfazed by sitting on the bench for the first time in his major league career, Piniella made the most of his infrequent appearances in the batting order, building off of a strong start to become an everyday fixture in the Yankee lineup. Piniella had been a model of consistency, keeping his batting average within a few points of .300 all season long.

As the baseball world said "Farewell" to the month of August it appeared that the tide in the American League eastern division strongly favored the Boston Red Sox. Upon the completion of play on August 29 the Sox held a relatively commanding lead of five games over the Yankees, seven and a half games over Cleveland, and a seemingly insurmountable eight game lead over the fourth place Orioles. Boston's Luis Tiant had already recorded his twentieth win and perennial star Carl Yastrzemski was having yet another outstanding season, but the club had suffered the loss of the irreplaceable Carlton Fisk in late June and was relying on a network of solid if unspectacular players to keep the lineup and the pitching staff afloat. In the absence of a hot streak by any of their divisional competitors, their patchwork lineup had played well enough to allow the Sox to maintain their lead atop the divisional standings. If the Red Sox could sustain their winning pace from August throughout the stretch drive, the divisional championship would be theirs.

With the arrival of Labor Day on September 2, all teams would play their divisional rivals through the end of the season. For the Red Sox that meant a trip to Baltimore for a Labor Day double header against the Orioles. The Red Sox entered this critical series on the heels of a brief two-game losing streak as they closed out play against the western division. In contrast, the Orioles wrapped up their western schedule with a solid four game winning streak. The standings favored the Red Sox, but the momentum was shifting toward Baltimore.

The Baltimore franchise had suffered a long history of mediocrity, first as the St. Louis Browns, and later as the newest incarnation of the Orioles. A rebuilding effort in the mid-1960s had rendered the club as the successor to the Yankees as one of the dominant teams in the league. The Orioles had earned four of the first five eastern division titles since the inception of divisional play in 1969, missing the fifth title by just five games. The hallmark of those great teams had been their dominant starting pitching, anchored by Jim Palmer, Dave McNally, and Mike Cuellar. Since coming together as a trio in 1969, the group had fifteen seasons of eighteen wins or more between them, including the incredible season of 1971 when the trio teamed with current Yankee Pat Dobson to become the first team in fifty years to feature four twenty game winners, a feat unlikely to be repeated in the future. For the 1974 season the Palmer-McNally-Cuellar trio was joined by newcomer Ross Grimsley, who quickly established himself as one of the top pitchers in the American League. The fact that three of the four star starters were left handed only added to their potential to dominate their competition. Fortunately for the rest of the division, ace Jim Palmer was suffering from a rare drop in performance which saw the star lose ten of his first fourteen decisions in an injury-plagued year. Like the Yankees, the Orioles had played steady baseball throughout the 1974 season but had been unable to put together an extended hot streak. Before sweeping the Kansas City Royals prior to the start of the Red Sox series the Orioles record was a game below .500. It was the latest point in the season that an Orioles team had been below .500 since 1967.

With the opportunity to bury the Orioles with a double header sweep, the Red Sox started their two ace pitchers, Luis Tiant and Bill Lee. The Orioles countered with Grimsley and Cuellar. This matchup of aces produced a predictable result – two nail-biting pitchers' duels. In the first game Tiant and Grimsley yielded just six hits and three walks between them as both went the distance. The only blemish was a fourth inning solo home run by Oriole second baseman Bobby Grich, resulting in a 1-0 Oriole win. Game two offered no similar fireworks (other than the ejection of Oriole Manager Earl Weaver). Once again the outcome was 1-0 in favor of the Orioles, with the only run scoring on a couple of singles, a couple of bunts, and a sacrifice fly, supported by a two hitter by Cuellar. In their last attempt to salvage a victory in the series the Red Sox went up against the previously struggling Jim Palmer. The righty delivered a vintage Jim Palmer performance, holding the Red Sox scoreless on just three hits for his first complete game victory since April. In three games against Oriole pitching the Sox had managed to scratch out only eight hits without scoring a single run or forcing the Orioles to go to their bullpen. Instead of burying the Orioles, the Red Sox were digging a hole for themselves. The losing streak would extend to eight games before the Sox finally took two games against the Brewers. What had looked like a clear path to a title was now a very twisted, bumpy road for the Red Sox.

Meanwhile, the Band on the Run Yankees had closed their western schedule with ten wins in their last eleven games. The reconfigured pitching rotation of Medich, Dobson, Tidrow, May, and Gura was performing like a well-oiled machine. Playing their own holiday double header against the Brewers, the Yankees continued their winning ways by taking their sixth straight game in the first game before losing a 3-2 heartbreaker in the nightcap as a result of a Chris Chambliss error that led to three unearned runs. The team rebounded by winning three of their next five, capped by a shutout by Larry Gura. At the close of play on September 8 the Yankees were locked in a first place tie with Boston as both teams sported identical 74-65 records. The Yankees headed to Boston for a short two game series at Fenway Park, perhaps the most critical series for the franchise since the incredible finish of 1964. Fenway Park had not been kind to the Yankees over the last three seasons. The team was winless in seven tries in Boston so far in 1974, and their record over the prior two seasons at Fenway was a miserable 3-15. Nevertheless the team was hot, they were loose, and they were playing with the confidence of a gambler playing with the house's money.

Game one of the battle for first place resulted in shining moments for two Yankees whose 1974 seasons had thus far been major disappointments. As a result of unmet high expectations and a big buildup by management, negative public comments from his new teammates, and a slow start in pinstripes, Chris Chambliss had found himself a target of the boo birds in the seats of Shea Stadium. Bill Virdon further complicated matters by platooning Chambliss with rookie Otto Velez and Bill Sudakis through much of the summer. Chambliss, billed as a future batting champion, found his batting average hovering just above the .200 mark during his first months in pinstripes. Chambliss rose above the pressure to heat up just in time for the stretch drive, posting a .327 batting average in the critical month of September. The lefty first baseman delivered a clutch home run while scoring a second run in the September 9 opener against the Red Sox. Veteran Roy White also contributed to the important Yankee victory. White opened that game in classic Roy White fashion – leading off the game by reaching on an error, stealing second and advancing to third on another error, then scoring on a Maddox single before scoring another run in the fifth inning. White had long been an unsung hero of the Yankee clubs during the CBS era. A second baseman in the minor leagues, he was inexplicably thrown into the outfield in one of manager Johnny

Keane's more bizarre maneuvers when White joined the club for a cup of coffee in September 1965. It was a move that resulted in an arm injury that haunted White for the remainder of his career. The team attempted to convert him to the hot corner, but eventually put him back into the outfield to stay. An outstanding spring and a meltdown by Yankee star of the future Steve Whitaker in 1968 resulted in White's rise as an unexpected fixture in the Yankee outfield. For the next six years White was arguably one of the most important contributors to the erratic Yankee offense, providing a stable combination of power, speed, and an ability to get on base. White would appear in two All-Star games and twice he would play an entire season without missing a game, most recently in 1973. But as with many of the fixtures from the prior regime, the new management team seemed to view White with contempt. After Gabe Paul failed in his efforts to replace him in the Yankee lineup, White began the 1974 campaign as the everyday left fielder. A slow start, a nagging hamstring injury, and the emergence of Maddox and Piniella largely reduced White to the role of designated hitter for the second half of the season. In the years to come White would continue to spend his winters reading of Yankee plans to replace him, only to win back his starting role in the spring. His contribution to the win over the Red Sox was one of the most satisfying of his difficult 1974 season. The fact that the Yankees were now the sole owners of first place was icing on the cake.

The next night provided an opportunity for two September reinforcements to make their most significant contribution to their new club. The game featured another classic pitching duel, with Yankee righty Pat Dobson facing Boston ace Luis Tiant in a game that would add another entry into the litany of controversial events that defined the contentious rivalry between the two clubs. The Sox scratched out a run in their half of the first courtesy of a Thurman Munson throwing error. The score remained 1-0 until the top of the ninth. Tiant was cruising along when he issued a one out walk to Lou Piniella. Virdon sent in rookie speedster Larry Murray to pinch run for the much slower Piniella. This was exactly the type of moment that Murray had been added to the roster for. Red hot Chris Chambliss drove a pitch into the right field corner, driving in the speedy Murray and landing Chambliss on third with a triple. This is where things got complicated. The umpires had observed that the ball had possibly bounced in and out of the hands of a fan, sparking a debate over whether or not the play should be ruled a ground rule double based upon interference by a fan with a ball in play and whether Murray should score or be forced to return to third base. The umpires ruled that the fan had interfered with the ball while it remained in play, pushing Chambliss back to second base with a ground rule double. Fortunately for the Yankees, the umpires also used their discretion to award Murray with home plate, tying the score. This umpire privilege is expressly permitted, is rarely exercised, and almost always results in a furious response by the team on the losing end of such a decision. On the latter point this night was no exception. In the ensuing twenty-five minute argument Red Sox manager Darrell Johnson was ejected and Chambliss was struck by a steel dart thrown from the stands, nearly causing a Red Sox forfeit. Order was restored, Tiant escaped the inning, with the game now tied 1-1. In light of Dobson's masterful performance, Virdon stuck with his pitcher through the ninth, tenth, and eleventh innings. Along the way he allowed the righty to weather two potentially game-winning rallies by the Red Sox. The first was a two-out, bases loaded jam in the bottom of the ninth. Despite the fact that the Red Sox had the winning run ninety feet away, two lefty hitters were due up, and the Yankees had a well-rested lefty bullpen trio of Sparky Lyle, Mike Wallace, and Tippy Martinez standing patiently by, Virdon stayed with Dobson. The lefties stayed in the bullpen again in the eleventh when the Red Sox put runners on first and second with two out and with lefty line drive hitter Cecil Cooper in the batter's box. A spectacular play on the outfield grass by Sandy Alomar ended the inning as the Yankees dodged another bullet fired against their starting pitcher. The deadlock continued into the twelfth inning when newcomer Alex Johnson hit a solo home run in just his second Yankee at bat to give the Yankees the lead. Dobson finally yielded to Lyle, who sealed the win by retiring all three hitters in the bottom of the inning, wrapping up the game by retiring rookie (and future Hall-of-Famer) Jim Rice. The remarkable ninth inning rally, the fantastic marathon performance by Dobson, and the heroic home run by the newly arrived Johnson made it the kind of victory that could easily lead a team to believe that they were a team of destiny and that all of the breaks were now falling their way.

September 10, 1974	W	L	T	PCT	GB
New York Yankees	76	65	0	.539	-
Baltimore Orioles	74	67	0	.525	2
Boston Red Sox	74	67	0	.525	2
Cleveland Indians	70	70	0	.500	5.5
Milwaukee Brewers	68	75	0	.476	9
Detroit Tigers	65	77	0	.458	11.5

In the Driver's Seat

Next on the Yankee agenda was a three game series against the revitalized Baltimore Orioles. The Orioles had followed their three shutouts against the fading Red Sox with two more shutouts against Cleveland, wrapping up the Cleveland series with one additional win to extend their winning streak to ten games. After suffering a minor setback by losing two of three to the Brewers, the Orioles prepared to host the Yankees with their club now just two games behind New York. With the Oriole pitchers hitting their peak at just the right time, the Yankee hold on first place might be short-lived and the Orioles, who just a couple of weeks before seemed destined to drop completely out of the pennant race, were in a position to take control of the standings.

The series began on September 11 with a twi-night double header. Both teams had played double headers earlier in the week, the Yankees had closed their previous series with the pressure-packed twelve inning win in Boston, and the Orioles had just played two consecutive extra-inning games against Milwaukee. The last thing these clubs needed was a mid-September nighttime double header, and the fatigue resulting from their heavy schedules would soon be compounded. The Yankees drew first blood by scoring two runs in the top of the second in the opener, with Alex Johnson again playing a major role. Rudy May gave up a single run in the bottom of the inning, and the Orioles tied the game in the fifth courtesy of a solo home run by weak hitting catcher Andy Etchebarren. From there the score remained knotted at 2-2 into the seventeenth inning. The Orioles had a chance to score the winning run in the seventh inning but found themselves on the losing end of an interference call that cost them a run and led to yet another ejection for manager Earl Weaver. As he had with Dobson a day earlier, Virdon allowed May to pitch beyond the ninth inning before replacing him with one out in the tenth with Sparky Lyle. The Yankee short man went on to pitch an incredible six and two-thirds innings of relief before being mercifully lifted in the seventeenth in favor of Cecil Upshaw. On the Baltimore side, Weaver (calling the shots from the clubhouse) stuck with starter Ross Grimsley for a remarkable fourteen innings. After numerous aborted rallies by both clubs, the Orioles finally scored the winning run off Upshaw in the seventeenth inning. It was already a long night, but the two teams still had another game to play.

Fortunately for both teams the nightcap was a much more traditional affair. Faced with a depleted pitching staff after playing thirty-eight innings over the last three days, Weaver turned to relief pitcher Don Hood to start the second game. The Yankees knocked the lefty out in the second inning with a four run rally on their way to a 5-1 victory. Larry Gura gave the bullpen a much needed game off and delivered yet another stellar performance. Thurman Munson caught all twenty-six innings in the double header, a grueling day's work that resulted in the durable and stubborn star relenting to a game off the next afternoon.

To close out the series Bill Virdon made one of the most unorthodox decisions of his Yankee managerial career by bypassing established starter Dick Tidrow in favor of little-used southpaw Mike Wallace. Wallace was a quirky character with a split-finger fastball that broke so sharply that the lefty had a great deal of trouble reliably throwing it for strikes. Serving almost exclusively as a middle reliever since being acquired in May for Ken Wright, Wallace had quietly put together a 5-0 mark by rescuing starting pitchers who were sent for early showers and then reaping the benefits of mid-game rallies that gave the Yankees the lead. The September 12 start was his first and only start of the season, with nothing less than first place on the line. The southpaw had earned a complete game victory in his major league debut over a year earlier, but since that time had never pitched more than four innings in a game. On this day he rewarded Virdon's insight and confidence by delivering a sensational scoreless performance through seven and two-thirds innings, giving the Yankees a 3-0 victory and dropping the Orioles back to third place, three games behind New York.

The next few games on the schedule favored the Yankees, who had the benefit of playing a three game series against the last place Detroit Tigers while the fatigued Orioles faced yet another double header against the Cleveland Indians to start a four game set in Baltimore. The Orioles reignited their hot hand by taking the first three games against the Indians before losing the fourth. The second game of their September 13 twi-night double header featured a classic Earl Weaver stunt. With rain falling and the Orioles ahead going into the seventh inning, Cleveland rallied in the top of the inning to take a 6-5 lead. As the rain continued, the umpires made the decision to call for the tarp to be put over the field. In the eyes of the Indians, Weaver's ground crew purposely stalled for time to allow as much rain as possible to accumulate. Under the rules of the time, if the field was rendered unplayable the score would revert back to what it had been at the end of the last full inning, which in this case would have given

Baltimore the victory. Cleveland filed a protest with the league office, and the teams waited for the rain to end and for the game to resume on the now sloppy field. When the game did resume the Orioles tied the score in their half of the seventh. Perhaps karma took a hand in that inning as veteran Oriole Tommy Davis tweaked his hamstring while running the bases after his game-tying home run. No doubt the two hour rain delay and the wet field had something to do with the injury, which proved to be mild and did not cost Davis much playing time. The game was suspended because of the league curfew and the clubs were forced to finish it the next day, with Baltimore winning by a final score of 8-6.

Meanwhile, the Yankees suffered an unfortunate setback. The club optimistically hoped to sweep Detroit, but had to settle for two victories after losing to the Tigers 6-3 in the opener. In the second game Dobson showed signs that he had not fully recovered from his eleven inning gem four days earlier, but a Bobby Murcer home run led the Yanks to a 10-7 comeback victory. The Yankees easily took the rubber game 10-2 behind Larry Gura's fourth win since joining the club and a four-hit performance by Lou Piniella.

All things considered the Yankees were flying high, having won eleven of sixteen games in the month of September. They were a team with very few players who had September pennant race or postseason experience, yet when the pressure was highest they had continued to play their best baseball of the season. There were just fifteen games left in the regular season, and although their two and a half game lead over the second place Orioles may not be a comfortable margin, it was far, far better to be two and a half games up with fifteen games left than two and a half games down. The fact that ten of those fifteen games would be played in their "home" park of Shea Stadium might have helped boost their already brimming confidence, although the club had actually played better on the road in September. The fact that the Orioles were now also playing their best baseball of 1974 was not helpful, but it was the Orioles who needed to make up ground while the Yankees had that two and a half game buffer to ease their minds.

It was with that backdrop that the Baltimore Orioles arrived in Flushing for the three game series that could decide the winner of the eastern division.

September 15, 1974	W	L	PCT	GB
New York Yankees	80	67	.544	-
Baltimore Orioles	78	70	.527	2.5
Boston Red Sox	76	70	.521	3.5
Cleveland Indians	72	74	.493	7.5
Milwaukee Brewers	71	77	.480	9.5
Detroit Tigers	67	80	.456	13

Nemesis

The last Yankee league championship in 1964 marked the beginning of an era of parity in the American League. From 1964-1968, five different teams took home the league's championship trophy. Thanks largely to the dominance of the Yankee franchise, this period of five different champions in five years was unprecedented in league history. The league had seen four different champions over a four year period twice before, but both of these instances (1904-1907 and 1918-1921) predated Yankee dominance over the standings. The 1964-1968 cycle was a particularly ominous omen for Yankee hopes of restoring their dynasty as traditional door mats like the Baltimore Orioles (descendants of the hapless St. Louis Browns who had a single league championship during their time in the league, with that sole World Series appearance coming during the chaotic World War II years) and the Minnesota Twins (descended from the original Washington Senators, with only three league championships in their first sixty-four years as a franchise) joining with traditional Yankee rivals Detroit and Boston to win league titles. In the following years the Oakland Athletics, another traditionally weak franchise coming off of decades at the bottom of the standings, would also rise to become a dominant force. This changing of the guard atop the standings added one more source of pressure on the Bronx Bombers as they tried to return to past glory. And of all these teams there was no greater thorn in the side of the Yankees than the Baltimore Orioles.

Success was largely elusive to the St. Louis Browns, and equally hard to come by for their successors after the latter's move to Baltimore in 1954. After finishing in third place in 1945, the best finish the

Browns/Orioles could muster over the next fifteen years was a fifth place finish in the eight team American League by the Orioles in 1957. Other than the World War II years, the Browns/Orioles had not finished over .500 a single time from 1930-1959, regularly finishing below the .400 mark and losing over a hundred games six times.

The fortunes of the Orioles began to shift began to shift in 1960 with the arrival of the Baby Birds, a name derived from a pitching staff that featured three twenty-one year-old and two twenty-two year-old starters. The general manager overseeing this youth movement was none other than future Yankee GM Lee MacPhail, who was in the process of honing his philosophy of patience and talent development with his young ballplayers. The upstart ball club with their patient GM, their youthful pitching staff, and a sweet fielding, twenty-three year-old third baseman named Brooks Robinson shocked the baseball world by holding the top spot in the 1960 standings into the middle of September. The Baby Birds folded in the final weeks of the season and the Yankees won nineteen of their last twenty-one games (including their last fifteen) to reestablish their dominance and take home the American League title. Still, the Orioles had delivered the message that they were a budding powerhouse and were no longer to be taken lightly.

The young Orioles continued to act as a solid contender in the American League as the decade of the sixties progressed. Many thought them to be the best team in the league in 1964 when their franchise record ninety-seven wins left them just two games shy of the resurgent Yankees. That would prove to be the last time that the Yankees bested the Orioles in the standings as the two clubs entered the 1974 season. The Orioles completed their emergence as a force in the American League by taking home the world championship in 1966. The club had largely followed general manager Lee MacPhail's belief that you could not build a winning team by trades, with the significant exception of a trade with the Cincinnati Reds in which the Orioles sent a package featuring pitcher Milt Pappas to the Reds in exchange for superstar Frank Robinson. Robinson, characterized by Reds GM Bill DeWitt as a player past his prime and on the precipice of a decline in performance, responded by winning the Triple Crown, leading the American League in batting, home runs, and runs batted in. With the two Robinsons, a deep pitching staff, and a seemingly endless stream of new talent rising from MacPhail's minor league development program, the Orioles would be an elite franchise for years to come. 1968 saw the arrival of new manager Earl Weaver and after finishing second that year the team reeled off three consecutive one hundred win seasons while winning one world championship and two additional American League titles. This juggernaut featured a lineup of All-Stars supported by one of the deepest starting pitching staffs in history. During this period the Birds outpaced the Yankees in the standings by an average of twenty-one games per season. Frustrated Yankee fans found their beloved club hopelessly overwhelmed by the Orioles, a reversal in fortune from what Browns and Orioles fans experienced during the Yankee heyday.

A few cracks in the Orioles armor began to emerge by 1972 as Frank Robinson was traded away and other stars from the team's dominant years began to show signs of age. To the great frustration of Yankee fans, the Orioles found a way to rebuild and retook the top spot in the division in 1973 behind newcomers like Bobby Grich and Don Baylor.

Yankee Resurrection

And so it was that the Baltimore Oriole club that arrived in Flushing with the mission of throwing cold water on the Yankee hot streak was a seasoned collection, confident and experienced with playing and winning important, pressure-filled games. The next few days would either give the Yankees and their fans the immense satisfaction of eliminating the hated Orioles as a threat to their pennant dreams or add one more chapter to the dark narrative that had hounded them for the past ten years.

Showdown

Having scored twenty runs in their last two games before the showdown series with the Orioles, the Yankees had good cause for optimism as they prepared to face one of the best pitching staffs in the game. Better still, the Yankees by this time had made Shea Stadium their true "home" field, with an entire season in Flushing under their belt. Having just beaten the Orioles in two out of three games on Baltimore's home turf, playing the Orioles at home for this critical series was a very positive factor in their favor. While in Detroit Bobby Murcer showed signs of breaking out of his season-long slump by hitting his first home run in a month and a half, and Nettles, Piniella, and Chambliss remained red hot at the plate. Still, the Oriole pitching staff was a key reason for the fact that the Orioles had waltzed to four of the last five eastern divisional titles. The three starting pitchers that would face the Yankees in the most critical series of the season, Jim Palmer, Mike Cuellar, and Dave McNally, were all former twenty game winners and all three had extensive experience in high pressure games, including nineteen World Series starts between them.

With the anticipated dominance of the starting pitching of both teams, it was no surprise that game one of the showdown series began with a pitcher's duel. For six innings Jim Palmer and Doc Medich held their opponents scoreless. Controversy erupted in the bottom of the sixth when the more experienced Orioles took advantage of the Yankees' relative inexperience in playing under pressure. Jim Mason led off the Yankee half of the sixth with a single. As expected, Sandy Alomar attempted to bunt

Mason to second. Alomar was the best on the team when it came to laying down a bunt, but this time he failed to get the ball onto the ground and instead popped it up to first baseman Boog Powell. Powell had the presence of mind to intentionally drop the ball. Once the ball hit the ground Powell picked it up and threw it to Bobby Grich, who touched first to retire Alomar and then tagged Mason, who had expected Powell to make the catch and was running back to first base. Yankee manager Virdon protested the game, arguing that Powell was not allowed to facilitate a double play by intentionally dropping the ball. Virdon and the Yankees later withdrew the protest when a review of the rules showed that the play by Powell, though unorthodox, was perfectly legal. The next inning the Orioles scored the game's first run on a double, a bunt single, and a sacrifice fly. The Orioles scored three more runs off of Medich and reliever Sparky Lyle in the eighth inning while Palmer continued to hold the Yanks scoreless, giving the Orioles a 4-0 victory.

In game two the Yankees started Pat Dobson while Weaver countered with Mike Cuellar. The teams had each scratched out two runs when the Orioles broke open the game by touching up Dobson, Dick Tidrow, and Mike Wallace for seven runs in the top of the sixth. The Yankees had their share of offense against Cuellar, producing twelve hits but scoring only four runs while leaving eight men on base. The Orioles held on for a final score of 10-4. Cuellar had his twentieth win and the Yankees had lost a significant portion of their hold on first place, facing the third and final game of the series with just a one-half game lead over the Orioles.

With the momentum swinging rapidly toward Baltimore, it fell to Rudy May to try to salvage a final victory against Oriole ace Dave McNally. May was good, as he held the Orioles to just one run and three hits over the first seven innings. Unfortunately for the Yankees, McNally was better as he scattered three hits and gave up no runs. The Orioles broke the game open in the eighth and tacked on six more runs against May, Cecil Upshaw, and the recently recalled Dave Pagan. The Yankees had squandered their lead in the standings, and for the first time since July 30 they had lost three games in a row. It could not have come at a worse time.

September 19, 1974	W	L	PCT	GB
Baltimore Orioles	81	70	.536	-
New York Yankees	80	70	.533	0.5
Boston Red Sox	77	72	.517	3
Cleveland Indians	73	75	.493	6.5
Milwaukee Brewers	72	78	.480	8.5
Detroit Tigers	69	81	.460	11.5

Desperate Times

It would have been easy for the Band on the Run to suffer a letdown after the pressure-packed series with the Orioles, particularly in light of the dismal outcome. But that was not this team's style and there were still critically important ballgames to be played. There was no time for head-hanging – the Yankees desperately needed victories.

After leaving New York, the rival Orioles headed north to Boston for a three game set. While the Red Sox had stumbled in recent weeks, they were still only three games behind the Orioles and were therefore a very motivated opponent. The Yankees, meanwhile, would play host for a four game series against a Cleveland Indian roster stacked with former Yankees who were eager to play spoiler against their former club. The Orioles added to the pressure on the Yankees by winning the opener against Boston on September 20.

The Cleveland series began with a double header in which the Indians would send legendary spitballer Gaylord Perry and former Yankee Fritz Peterson to the mound against Dick Tidrow and Larry Gura. Perry was in the midst of one of his finest seasons, and Peterson had gleefully notched two victories over his former teammates since the April trade to Cleveland. The first game of the twin bill was a seesaw affair which the Yankees won in a dramatic fashion when Murcer hit a walk off triple against Perry in the bottom of the ninth to score Elliot Maddox and give Sparky Lyle the win in relief of Tidrow.

The second game featured what was now becoming a typical Larry Gura performance. The man that neither the Cubs nor the Rangers considered good enough for the major leagues won his fifth game in a row, scattering six hits while walking only one batter in a masterful shutout. A few years earlier Cubs manager Leo Durocher criticized Gura for "not challenging hitters." By striking out only a single batter in his shutout, Gura demonstrated to the naysayers that a pitcher did not need overpowering speed to succeed at the major league level. Quite unexpectedly, Larry Gura was now one of the most critical contributors to the Yankee pennant race effort. Peterson and Fred Beene pitched well for Cleveland, but the hot Yankee hitters pushed across three runs to secure a 3-0 victory. The double header sweep put the Yankees back into a first place tie with the Orioles.

September 21 was a good day for the Yankees. Roy White kicked off his best game of the season by stealing home to give the Yankees a 1-0 lead in the first inning. Working with a 2-0 lead in the third, Medich imploded and the Indians scored seven runs against the Yankee ace and reliever Mike Wallace. In the bottom of the fourth Bobby Murcer capped a four run rally with his first Shea Stadium home run. It had taken seventy-seven games, but Murcer had finally broken the Shea curse. The Yanks continued the rally with four more runs in the fifth and another three in the seventh for a final score of 14-7. Rudy May continued his remarkable contribution to the Yankees by pitching a near perfect four and a third innings of relief for the win. Up north in Boston, the Orioles had endured three rain delays totaling three and a half hours to build a commanding 5-1 lead over the Red Sox in the bottom of the ninth inning when the Sox busted loose for four runs to tie the game. The Sox won the game in the bottom of the tenth. Red Sox pitcher Bill Lee pitched the entire game, which, including the three rain delays, took almost seven hours to complete. Said the quirky Lee about his marathon performance, "I went through four T-shirts, three uniforms, and three jars of Capsulin (a topical pain reliever). I also played three hours of bridge." The Yankees were once again in sole possession of first place, one game ahead of Baltimore and four ahead of the Red Sox with just nine games left to play.

The division leading Yankees closed out their series with the Indians on September 22. Pat Dobson had been largely ineffective since his jewel of a game at Fenway Park twelve days earlier, but on this day he was back in spectacular form and took a three-hitter and a 2-1 lead into the ninth inning. The Indians had the tying and winning runs on base with two outs when Sparky Lyle came in to secure the victory. Bobby Murcer drove in the winning run with his second Shea Stadium home run in as many days. The Yankees had survived a bonehead play by Piniella, who, believing that he had been called out on a play at second base but unaware that the fielder had dropped the ball and the umpire had reversed the call, stepped off the base and was tagged out. When it was all over the Yankee lead over Baltimore remained at one game as the O's defeated the Red Sox in the final game of their series. The Yankees were still, for at least the time being, in control of their own destiny.

It was at this point that the schedule favored the second place Orioles, who would face last place Detroit in five of their last eight games and fifth place Milwaukee in the other three. Meanwhile, the Yankees were due to face third place Boston and fourth place Cleveland for three games each, finishing their season with two games in Milwaukee. In addition to the schedule-maker, the Yankees were also battling the weatherman. The cancellation of the second game of an early August double header required the Yankees to double up with the Red Sox in the opener of the final scheduled series at Shea Stadium on September 24. The Yankee pitching staff, taxed by the stream of critical games in the prior weeks, could ill afford the requirement to serve up two quality starting pitchers on a single day. In the first game of the twin bill the Yankees called on Rudy May, who had not started in five days but had delivered that pressure-filled four-plus inning relief effort just three days earlier. May was roughed up for four runs, but it really didn't matter since Red Sox ace Luis Tiant held the Yankees scoreless. In game two Larry Gura proved that he was fallible, and the Red Sox completed a sweep of the double header. In addition to being outscored 8-2 in the doubleheader, the Yankees uncharacteristically made a total of four errors, including two by shortstop Jim Mason, and also suffered another base running blunder in the second game when Bobby Murcer was tagged out when he slipped after rounding second on a double. While the Yankees were losing two games to the Sox, the Orioles were spoiling the Tiger's celebration of Al Kaline's 3000th hit by coming from behind to beat ace reliever John Hiller with an eighth inning rally. The Orioles had regained control over the standings with a new half-game lead over the Yankees.

The Yankee fortunes seemed ready to reverse themselves a day later as Doc Medich delivered a ten-inning complete game victory over the Red Sox in the final regular season game in Shea Stadium. Elliott Maddox delivered the walk off single in the bottom of the tenth to give Medich his nineteenth win of the season. Red Sox lefty Bill Lee, pitching on just three day's rest after his remarkable seven hour performance in Boston, went the distance into extra innings again for the Red Sox. While the Yankees were winning in thrilling fashion, it had appeared that the Tigers were about to slow the Oriole momentum. Taking a 4-2 lead into the ninth inning with John Hiller, the league's best relief pitcher, waiting in the wings, Tiger manager Ralph Houk stayed with starter Mickey Lolich as the Orioles chipped away at the lead in the bottom of the ninth, eventually stealing a 5-4 victory. A chance for the Yankees to regain the top spot in the standings had slipped through their fingers.

The Yankees sat helpless on September 27 as rain prevented the start of their three game series in Cleveland. Although the rainout would give the pitching staff another day to rest, it would force another double header the following day. While the Yankees sat, the Orioles opened their series with Milwaukee with another classic pitcher's duel. Starters Jim Colborn and Jim Palmer matched each other zero for zero through twelve innings, at which point Palmer yielded to reliever Bob Reynolds. Colborn persevered through the thirteenth inning before likewise yielding to his bullpen. The game remained scoreless until the bottom of the seventeenth, when the Orioles loaded the bases with one out. Bob Oliver hit a slow roller to Brewer third baseman Don Money who was unable to get the out at home. The Orioles had another improbable victory and the Yankees were now a full game out of first place with five games left to play. The margin of error was getting thinner.

The next day it was the Orioles turn to wait as the Yankees battled Cleveland in their double header. For the Yankees it was now Ron Blomberg's time to shine. The twenty-five year-old designated hitter was still one of the best hitters in the game, but his lackluster defense was incompatible with the defensive-minded Bill Virdon, leaving Blomberg the odd man out in Virdon's lineup. Earlier in the season Virdon had Blomberg in the lineup every day, including against left handed pitching, and Blomberg responded with a respectable .276 average against southpaws while keeping his overall average above .300 for the entire season. With Lou Piniella, Elliott Maddox and Bobby Murcer playing every day in the outfield, Blomberg had been relegated to a part-time designated hitter role since mid-July. His start in the first game of the twin bill was his first opportunity to start a game in almost three weeks. Showing no signs of rust, Blomberg touched up starter Gaylord Perry for two home runs on the way to a 9-3 Yankee victory. In the eighth inning of the nightcap Blomberg came off the bench to hit a game-tying two run pinch hit home run off of former Yankee Fred Beene, followed by a two run homer by Roy White. The 9-7 victory gave the Yankees a much needed sweep and shifted the pressure to Baltimore. Once again the Birds responded, easily handing the Brewers a 7-1 defeat. The Yankees had shaved a half game off of the Oriole lead, but Baltimore still held a one-half game lead in the standings and a lead of a full game in the loss column.

The next day Baltimore again kept up the pressure on the Yankees by collecting yet another win. In this one, the Brewers and Orioles were tied 3-3 going into the bottom of the ninth. At that point Brewer starter Jim Slaton walked three Orioles to load the bases with one out. Ace reliever Tom Murphy coaxed a ground ball from Rich Coggins, but the speedy Coggins beat the relay at first after the runner at third was forced at home. Murphy then walked Boog Powell, forcing home the winning run and giving the Orioles yet another thrilling victory. The Yankees responded with a 10-0 pasting of Fritz Peterson and the Indians. As satisfying as the victory was, the Yankees could not afford to go win-for-win with the Orioles – Baltimore would have to eventually lose a game if the Yankees were to go to the postseason. But Baltimore refused to lose, and time was running out. The Orioles easily beat Ralph Houk's Detroit Tigers 12-6 during the Yankees final off day of the season on September 30. This left the Yankees with little chance for winning the division outright. With each team having but two remaining games and with the Orioles holding a one game lead, New York would need to win both games in Milwaukee with the Orioles losing their two remaining games in Detroit for the Yankees to win the division. And the way the Orioles were playing the chances for a Tiger sweep seemed remote. The Yankees would need a miracle.

September 30, 1974	W	L	PCT	GB
Baltimore Orioles	89	71	.556	-
New York Yankees	88	72	.550	1
Boston Red Sox	83	77	.519	6
Cleveland Indians	76	84	.475	13
Milwaukee Brewers	75	85	.469	14
Detroit Tigers	72	88	.450	17

Fight at the Pfister

Instead of receiving the benefit of a miracle from above, the Yankees created a disaster from within.

Despite the mounting odds against them, the Band on the Run was leaving Cleveland on a high note. They needed to sweep the Indians and they had done just that. The team was riding high, but the pressure level was high as well. After five months of flirting with the .500 mark, the Orioles had gone 26-6 and were now in control of their own destiny. If the Yankees were to proceed to the postseason they would need to play their very best baseball in Milwaukee. In addition, they had to hope that Ralph Houk's desire to play spoiler against the Orioles outweighed any vindictive feelings toward his former employers, as the Yankees desperately needed their former skipper's last place club to turn the tide on the Orioles momentum.

The bad weather that had plagued the start of the Indian series lingered as the Yankees prepared to board their flight to Milwaukee to compete in the final series of the regular season. Flights out of Cleveland were delayed, leaving the ballplayers with little to do but wait out the three hour delay as best they could. They were a group of thirty-odd young men working under intense pressure. Not surprisingly, a few post-game drinks in the clubhouse were followed by a few drinks at the airport bar, which were followed by a few more drinks when the flight to Milwaukee finally took off.

Of the twenty-five men who had broken camp with the Yankees six months earlier, only fifteen remained. Among those fifteen were backups Bill Sudakis and Rick Dempsey. The two players had enjoyed a total of only fourteen at bats between them during the month of September and neither was happy about the lack of an opportunity to contribute. With that simmering frustration as a backdrop, the two players had engaged in an animated, two-way battle of verbal jousting throughout the elongated trip from Cleveland to Milwaukee. When Sudakis threw firecrackers into the aisle of the team bus on the way from the airport to Milwaukee's Pfister Hotel, Dempsey's temper boiled over and threats were exchanged between the two players. Accounts vary as to what transpired next. One story has Dempsey and Sudakis entering the revolving door together and emerging on the other side in a full scale battle. Another has Sudakis asking Dempsey to choose whether he wanted a beating with boxing gloves or bare knuckles, prompting Dempsey to unleash a savage beating on Sudakis. Whatever the ignition source, the battle was on between the two. Coach Mel Wright was joined by Thurman Munson, Walter Williams, Mike Wallace, Sparky Lyle, and Bobby Murcer in an attempt to separate the two combatants. With lobby furniture flying and a pile of athletes on the floor, order was eventually restored. This was not an ordinary baseball fight, with a little pushing and shoving and no harm done. Rick Dempsey was described as apoplectic, requiring multiple teammates to restrain him. The conflict was so violent that peacemaker Bobby Murcer had actually lost a shoe in the melee.

At first it was believed that there were no serious consequences to the lobby fight. The first report was that damage was limited to lobby furniture and a pair of sunglasses belonging to Murcer. Bill Sudakis was rumored to be badly injured, but he had started only one game in the entire month of September and was not expected to be in the lineup against

Milwaukee anyway. The players went to their rooms, and Bill Virdon told reporters the he would handle disciplinary actions, if any, privately. As the evening ended the Yankee traveling staff quietly addressed the issue with the hotel and all appeared to be well. Unknown to anyone at the time, the fight was about to have a dire consequence for the team's postseason dreams. Bobby Murcer awoke the next morning to find that he could not move a finger he had jammed as he tried to separate the combatants the night before. An evaluation by the training staff confirmed the worst case scenario – the finger was broken and Murcer would not be available for the most important two games of his career.

The best label for Bobby Murcer's 1974 season would be "complicated." He had begun the year on the wrong side of Gabe Paul and with the perception by Steinbrenner and Paul that he was overpaid and underperforming. Then came the preseason scuttlebutt about the probable impact of Shea Stadium on Murcer's power production and the subsequent decline in Murcer's home run output. This was compounded by Murcer's demotion from center field to right field in favor of Elliot Maddox. On the actual playing field, the story was also complicated. Although it was true that Murcer's home park home run production had dropped from nineteen in 1973 to two during his first year at Shea, he batted a robust .302 at Shea in contrast to a .248 average on the road. After heating up and playing a large role in carrying the team through July and August, Murcer hit a disappointing .232 during the critical month of September. All of this was a prelude to the most critical two games of the season – if Murcer had closed out the season on a high note and led the Yankees to victory, much of the baggage of the season would be relieved. Instead he would have to watch the season finale from the bench and the Yankees would need to find a way to compensate for his absence.

Win or Go Home

One of the bright spots of the Yankee 1974 season was the defensive performance of their outfield. To say that this was a most unexpected development would be an understatement. The Opening Day alignment of Roy White, Bobby Murcer, and Ron Blomberg was not one that would suggest that outfield defensive prowess would be a Yankee strength. At that point few, if any, pundits had taken into account the presence of Elliot Maddox and the tenacity of Bill Virdon. Virdon himself was a glove master, having snagged a Gold Glove Award in 1962 along side of two pretty good outfielders named Willie Mays and Roberto Clemente. His Yankee spring training outfield drills had become the stuff of legend, and they had paid off. Murcer had also won a Gold Glove in 1972, but most observers credited that award to Murcer's offense and high profile (neither of which is supposed to influence Gold Glove Award voting). Murcer was generally regarded as an above average center fielder at best. The move to right field relieved the pressure on Murcer to anchor the outfield and he did settle in among the best right fielders in the league. Maddox was sensational in center, as Virdon had expected when he made the move. Lou Piniella became the primary left fielder, forcing Roy White into the designated hitter role. While not as dramatic a move as the shift of Murcer from center to right, the removal of White from left field, the position at which he had started all 162 games a season before, was another departure from the Yankee past. Observers regularly complimented Piniella on his improved defense in left field, which was widely seen as a tribute to Virdon's tutelage and Piniella's work ethic and an upgrade over White. The three Yankee outfielders unexpectedly found themselves as the top three in outfield assists in the American League. Now the absence of Murcer from the lineup in Milwaukee forced a change in the winning outfield formula. White, despite having played left field only a handful of times since his move to the designated hitter role in mid-July, would be pressed back into service while Piniella was shifted to right field. Although Piniella had never played right field at the major league level prior to his trade to the Yankees, he had started thirty-two games there during the season. Unfortunately, only two of those starts had come since he replaced White in left field in July. Despite the improvement in Piniella's defensive performance under Virdon he was still not the kind of player who could easily shift from one corner outfield position to another with limited opportunity to adjust. With lefty Kevin Kobel starting for the Brewers, Alex Johnson would slide into the designated hitter spot vacated by White. It would be Johnson's third start since joining the team, and his first start in three weeks. The lineup was far from ideal for one of the most important games of the season, but it was the best lineup that the Yankees could field under the circumstances.

With the season on the line Virdon turned to his most consistent pitcher throughout the 1974 campaign, Doc Medich. Medich was well rested, with five days off since his ten inning shutout of the Red Sox. The Brewer lineup that he would face was with a single exception filled with regulars, eager to play spoiler against the contender. With a one hour time difference in Milwaukee and the Orioles scheduled to play a day game in Detroit against the Tigers, the Yankees would know exactly where they stood as they took the field with their backs against the wall.

In their quest to clinch at least a tie in the final standings, the Orioles turned to Jim Palmer for the start against the Tigers. The Tigers gave the scoreboard-watching Yankees immediate cause for hope by jumping off to a 2-0 lead in the first inning. The Orioles fought back and took a 6-4 lead into the bottom of the eighth inning. The Tigers rallied to tie the game in the eighth, a rally triggered by the final major league hit by Al Kaline. The seesaw battle went into the top of the ninth when Houk brought in star reliever John Hiller to try to hold off the Orioles. Baltimore scored the go-ahead run when Andy Etchebarren hit a pinch hit double that scored slow footed Brooks Robinson all the way from first base. The Tigers put the tying run on third base with two outs in their half of the ninth, but Al Kaline took a called third strike and the game was over. The Orioles had clinched a tie, and the Yankees now needed to win both of the remaining two games in Milwaukee to extend their Cinderella season.

With a jury-rigged telephone connection to Milwaukee, the Orioles kept close tabs on the Yankee progress against the Brewers. At first they did not like what they heard. Medich scattered four hits over the first six innings while Kobel also held the Yankees scoreless. An Elliott Maddox RBI triple was followed by an Alex Johnson single in the seventh, and the Yankees had a 2-0 lead. With Medich at the top of his game and a well-rested bullpen, there was every reason to expect that the Yankees would survive to extend their chances for a share of first place to the last game of the season. It was at this point that the Yankee outfield felt the absence of Bobby Murcer. With one out in the bottom of the eighth, rookie pinch hitter Bob Hansen sliced a line drive toward right center field. It would have been a difficult catch for Bobby Murcer, but one that he would have likely made. Unfortunately, Lou Piniella was not Bobby Murcer. As is not unusual for someone playing a corner outfield position that they are not used to, Piniella initially broke in the wrong direction when the ball left Hansen's bat. By the time he recovered the ball was in the gap and Hansen was on third with a triple. The incident would cause Piniella to recall that his nemesis Earl Weaver had once predicted that Piniella would one day "screw up in the outfield" to the benefit of Weaver's Orioles. That time had indeed come. Don Money followed with a sinking line drive to center. Maddox risked everything to try a shoestring catch and lost – the ball skipped by him for another triple. A sacrifice fly tied the game, and it remained tied into the Brewer half of the tenth inning. Though his entire bullpen was available, Virdon sent Medich out once again in the extra frame. Rookie Jack Lind, the only player in the Brewer line up who had not been a regular during the season, opened the inning with a double. It was one of only five hits that Lind would accumulate in the major leagues. Still, Virdon left Medich on the mound. Light hitting John Vukovich sacrificed Lind to third. Medich remained in the game, intentionally walking Don Money to set up a potential inning ending double play. Medich still remained on the mound. Medich surrendered an unintentional walk to Sixto Lezcano to load the bases. Virdon still made no move to replace Medich. George Scott hit a game-winning single, and the Band on the Run was eliminated from pennant contention.

With a trip to the postseason now out of reach the Yankees wrapped up their 1974 campaign by beating the Brewers on the last day of the season. Ron Blomberg took over for the ailing Murcer in right field and September call up Terry Whitfield started in center field in place of

Elliott Maddox. For Maddox the rest was more than just a well-deserved day off after a tiring stretch drive. Maddox had thrilled Yankee fans with his phenomenal play in center field down the stretch, starting fifty-nine of the team's last sixty games. What those fans did not know was that Maddox was playing with a painful hernia, a condition finally addressed by postseason surgery.

The absence of Murcer, the misplay by Piniella, and the ill-fated decision to rely on Medich to work out of trouble in the tenth inning all provided fodder for Monday morning quarterbacks, but the truth was that the Yankees had spun their wheels for too long early in the season and the Orioles had peaked higher than the New Yorkers down the stretch, finishing their season with a nine game winning streak. Both clubs won on the final day of the season, leaving the Yankees two games out of first place. The club would split a second place reward of $48,579.27 between them, amounting to a $1,302.92 check for every player and coach who had earned a full share. That check and a promise of "Wait until next year" signaled the end of the improbable pennant run of the 1974 Yankees.

The Yankees and their fans were not alone in their disappointment – all four divisional races had come down to the last week, and in the National League east the Pirates clinched their title over the Cardinals on the very last day of the season. The first ten American League divisional races since the introduction of divisional play in 1969 had been decided by an average of ten games. Having two close American League races in 1974 was the best gift yet for the fathers of divisional play. The Yankees 89-73 record would have landed the club in second place in the western division, one game behind Oakland. That same record was one win better than manager Bill Virdon's former Pirates club accumulated while winning the National League eastern division title by a game and a half. None of these facts did anything to remove the sting felt throughout Yankeeland.

With his hex on Lou Piniella behind him and the Yankees out of the picture, Earl Weaver led his sizzling hot Orioles into the American League Championship Series against the two-time defending world champion Oakland Athletics. After capturing the first game of the series for their tenth win in a row and their twenty-ninth win in their last thirty-five games, the Orioles were held to a single run in the last three games of the playoff series and the A's returned to the World Series for the third straight season. Baltimore's amazing season had come to a close.

The loss to the Athletics ended Baltimore's mini-dynasty – during a nine-year period from 1966-1974 the Orioles won two world championships, two additional American League championships, and two additional eastern divisional championships. The descendants of the St. Louis Browns, whose lack of success in the early decades of the century mirrored that of the early New York Highlanders/Yankees, had enjoyed an almost Yankeelike run as one of the top teams in baseball but that run was over. The club would not return to the postseason until 1979, following that appearance with a world championship in 1983. As of this writing they have not appeared in a World Series since.

October 2, 1974 (FINAL)	W	L	PCT	GB
Baltimore Orioles	91	71	562	-
New York Yankees	89	73	549	2
Boston Red Sox	84	78	519	7
Cleveland Indians	77	85	475	14
Milwaukee Brewers	76	86	469	15
Detroit Tigers	72	90	444	19

Recognition

Few baseball insiders expected the New York Yankees to make a serious run at the 1974 divisional title. By that definition, the team had overachieved. Overachievement has its benefits. Among the awards distributed at the end of a baseball season are the awards given to the game's Manager and Executive of the Year. These awards typically go to winners of championships or leaders whose ball clubs have significantly exceeded expectations. It was this latter category that had elevated manager Bill Virdon and President Gabe Paul as the Major League Manager and Major League Executive of the Year for 1974. Among some veteran Yankee players, the recognition for the much-hated Paul and the laisse fare Virdon was viewed with derision. The selection of Virdon was seen as incredibly ironic by some players who believed that Virdon's management of the pitching staff and minimalist attitude toward in-game strategy were more of an impediment to success than awardable attributes. Clearly, the award voters felt otherwise. After being fired just a year earlier, and after enduring the indignity of the second choice label, Bill Virdon was now recognized as the most successful man in his profession. For their part, the Yankees recognized Virdon's success in a far more practical manner by giving him a new two-year contract.

While Bill Virdon was basking in the spotlight of recognition for his team's late season surge, the man who was the Yankees' first choice as manager was facing hard times in his fallback role as manager of the California Angels. The Angel team that Dick Williams took over at midseason was in last place in the American League's western division, and that is where they finished. The club finished in last place again in what would be his only full season as manager in 1975, and they were again hopelessly mired in last place when Williams was fired midway through the 1976 season.

Virdon's predecessor was also caught in the grip of hard managerial times. Ralph Houk's Tigers ended up at the bottom of the eastern division standings in 1974 and landed in that same position a year later. The veteran manager would not enjoy a winning season with the Tigers until his fifth and final year in 1978. Ironically, the Houk/Yankee story was not quite over when the 1974 season ended. While Houk continued to retain a high level of affection in the hearts of the dwindling number of Yankee players who remained from his managerial days, his reputation with the Yankee front office remained tarnished. The relationship another blow when certain members of the Yankee organization harshly criticized Houk for his team's inability to cool off the red hot Orioles in the final critical series of the season. Accusing Houk of having (at best) poor managerial judgement and (at worst) rolling over to the Orioles to spite his former employers, the ever diplomatic Major responded by noting that the Yankees had been swept at home by those same Orioles and that they had nobody but themselves to blame for their second place finish. The incident marked yet another unfortunate low point that marred the long career that Houk had enjoyed with the New York Yankees. In later years Mr. Steinbrenner would brush off criticism that he was callous and unfair to the many managers that he fired by claiming that he maintained excellent and cordial relations with his former field skippers, retaining many of them on his staff in various roles. Whatever truth there might have been in that position, it certainly did not describe the case of Ralph Houk.

PART FOUR

BACK WHERE WE BELONG

Two Games

Two games. The Yankees just needed to win two more games to complete the journey back to the postseason. The quantum leap forward in 1974 had fallen two games short and the team needed to find a way to upgrade their talent by at least the amount needed to win two more games the next season. Not a daunting task, but where and when to begin? It didn't take Gabe Paul long to take the first step, and to Yankees fans it made the Friday Night Massacre seem like a slight distraction. Just five days after the conclusion of the 1974 World Series, Gabe Paul shocked Yankee fans by trading Bobby Murcer.

Neither Gabe Paul nor George Steinbrenner shared Yankee fans reverence for Murcer. They viewed him as an overpaid, underperforming link to the declinasty years. The passing of the torch from Mickey Mantle to Murcer meant little to Paul, who could see only Murcer's sub-par 1974 performance and inflated salary. Rumors that Murcer was being shopped to other clubs persisted through the 1974 season but were not taken seriously by Yankee watchers. The beginning of the end of Murcer's time in pinstripes finally came during the 1974 World Series when Yankee brass were observed sitting alongside of their counterparts from San Francisco. It was reported that the discussions centered on Yankee interest in Bobby Bonds. The Yankees saw in Bonds the right handed power hitter that they had coveted for decades. With Bonds anchoring their lineup the Yankees would at last have someone who could provide the cadre of left handed Yankee power hitters with protection from the stream of left handed pitching frequently thrown against them. The rumored negotiations between New York and San Francisco came to a head less than a week after the conclusion of the Series when it was announced that the Yankees had acquired Bonds in exchange for Bobby Murcer in what was the first ever one-for-one trade of $100,000 ballplayers. Gabe Paul made the trade despite a hollow promise made by Steinbrenner that Bobby Murcer would be a Yankee as long as the Boss was there. The news was sprung on Murcer by Paul in an early morning telephone call on October 22. Paul told Murcer that the team had "decided to go in another direction." He seemed to relish delivering the news to the shocked ballplayer. "I have some news for you," Paul told the shocked Murcer, "and I hope you'll think it is good news."

Murcer did not consider this bombshell "good news." In fact, he later compared the impact of learning that he was leaving the Yankees to the news many years later that he had a brain tumor, even declaring in his autobiography that news of the trade had shocked him more than the cancer diagnosis. Yankee fans were also shaken by the news. Though Murcer had an off year and had missed the most critical series of the season due to a ridiculous injury, he was still arguably the most loved player on the club by a generation of fans who had little else to cheer for and who flocked to him upon his return from military service in 1969.

Once the news had sunk into the collective conscience of Yankee fans that the trade was a done deal and nothing would change it, a different perspective set in. In the discussion of the best all-around players in the game, the name Bobby Bonds was always mentioned as a top candidate for that title. Bonds was a classic five-tool player who could hit for average, hit for power, run like the wind, field his position with the best in the game, and who had a cannon for an arm. The primary, and accurate, criticism of him was that he struck out too much, and like Murcer his production had declined significantly in 1974. But Bonds seemed healthy, and at the age of twenty-nine appeared to be poised for a return to his previous form with the promise of a long and productive career in pinstripes. Maybe, just maybe, this would be the two-game upgrade that the team needed to reach the top. In fact, if you believe in the Wins Above Replacement (WAR) formula, Bonds 1974 WAR of 4.3 bested Murcer's WAR of 1.0 to the point that this trade alone would theoretically deliver more than the two additional wins that the Yankees needed.

But the Yankees were not done just yet...

Just as Bobby Bonds topped the charts as the most highly respected hitter in the game, Jim "Catfish" Hunter garnered similar respect as one of the top pitchers in the game. Coming off a Cy Young Award season with the world champion Oakland Athletics, Hunter had just enjoyed his fourth straight season of winning twenty-one or more games. The A's knew Hunter's value, and ordinarily he and his 6.9 WAR would not be available at any price. But this was not an ordinary situation. Oakland owner Charlie Finley had failed to make contractually required payments into an annuity fund for Hunter. In response, Hunter used a recently enacted collective bargaining grievance procedure to demand the full payment, interest on the missed payments, and termination of Hunter's obligation to remain with the Athletics. The labor arbiter agreed to all of his demands. Catfish Hunter was now a free agent, available to sign with any club he chose. His choice would be heavily influenced by money, and money was one thing that Mr. Steinbrenner had in abundance. While the acquisitions of players like Jim Mason, Pat Dobson, and Elliott Maddox showed the extent to which Steinbrenner would use his fortune to gather the talent necessary to improve his team, these situations were generally limited to the acquisition of lesser role players than for big stars. The Hunter case, a rare opportunity to bid for a top talent in the years prior to the arrival of broader free agency, gave Steinbrenner the opportunity to flex his financial muscles and score a huge win for his team.

The courtship of Hunter was intense, with other new money owners like San Diego Padres owner Ray Kroc willing to spend big bucks to secure the instant pitching staff upgrade that Hunter offered. In the end it was a combination of Steinbrenner's money and the engagement of Hunter confidant and Yankee scout Clyde Kluttz in the negotiation that swung Hunter's decision in the Yankees favor. With the stroke of a pen, Catfish Hunter had become the ace of the Yankee pitching staff and George Steinbrenner had the added satisfaction of scoring a blow against Charlie Finley, his protagonist a year earlier in the Dick Williams affair.

To Yankee fans, the Bonds and Hunter acquisitions served as a microcosm of the new Steinbrenner regime. The bitter shock of parting with the beloved modern face of the franchise was offset by the addition of two of the game's top players. The new regime's willingness to tear down Yankee tradition and feed an insatiable appetite to deliver a winning team resulted in conflicted feelings in the hearts of the pinstripe faithful. But at the end of the day all would be largely forgiven if it resulted in another pennant flying above Yankee Stadium.

Yankee Resurrection

The addition of Catfish Hunter had the unfortunate consequence of contributing to the conclusion of Mel Stottlemyre's career as a Yankee pitcher. Stottlemyre was not only no longer the ace of the staff, he was arguably the number five or six pitcher on the depth chart, even in the unlikely event that he fully recovered from his shoulder injury. Candidates for the 1975 Yankee rotation featured the reigning Cy Young Award winner Hunter backed by nineteen game winners Pat Dobson and Doc Medich. Since all three were, like Stottlemyre, right handed, a lefty was needed to break up the rotation and Rudy May was the clear choice in that regard. With fellow lefty Larry Gura coming off a spectacular September and righties Dick Tidrow and Dave Pagan competing for a spot at the back of the rotation, it was hard to see where even a healthy Stottlemyre would fit in. Full recovery was also a very improbable outcome. Stottlemyre had been diagnosed with a torn rotator cuff, and the nature of the tear was such that any attempt to repair it surgically would permanently end any chance Stottlemyre had of returning to the pitcher's mound. Stottlemyre's only hope was to completely rest the shoulder, let the tear heal naturally to the best extent possible, and then gently ease back into pitching form. Gabe Paul fired a shot across Stottlemyre's bow with a harbinger of things to come by threatening to cut Stottlemyre's salary by 20%, the maximum allowed under the rules of the time. It was a tactic that was particularly shocking given Stottlemyre's history with the team and the fact that he was rehabilitating from an injury, but quite typical for the Smiling Cobra. Stottlemyre threatened to take the team to salary arbitration, and eventually negotiated an agreement that would maintain his $90,000 salary if he was healthy enough to pitch by May 1, with the proposed 20% cut if he was not. Stottlemyre was promised by Gabe Paul that the May 1 milestone was his critical date and that he should not risk his full recovery by pushing too hard during spring training. Stottlemyre slowly began to work the shoulder into the best shape possible, refraining from appearing in any spring training games. Stottlemyre was discretely warned by friend, former teammate, and current Yankee pitching coach Whitey Ford that "some people were after him," but with the May 1 target date still a month away the veteran was completely caught off guard by a call to attend an impromptu meeting with Gabe Paul on March 31. It was at that meeting that Paul told the thirty-three year-old pitcher that he had been released. Stottlemyre reminded Paul of his promise to give the pitcher until May 1 to determine if he could return to action, but Paul was unmoved. Stottlemyre later learned that by releasing him on March 31 the Yankees were obligated to pay Stottlemyre only a small severance, saving them tens of thousands of dollars. Mel Stottlemyre never forgave Paul for his duplicity and essentially boycotted the Yankees before returning to pinstripes as Joe Torre's pitching coach over twenty years later. Stottlemyre received a kind offer from Ralph Houk to come and work out in an extended spring training with the Tigers. Stottlemyre accepted the opportunity, but pushed the shoulder too hard and reinjured it, permanently ending any hope of a comeback. Mel Stottlemyre's illustrious playing career was over.

The addition of Bonds and Hunter was justifiable cause for unbridled optimism in Yankeeland and the prevailing belief was that winning the 1975 eastern division title was a foregone conclusion. The team entered the season with minor concerns about the lack of production at second base, but the Oakland A's had just won three consecutive world championships with a rotating squad of light-hitting second basemen so it did not seem like a fatal weakness. With the addition of Hunter and Bonds, the assumption that players like Piniella, Maddox, Dobson, and Medich could repeat their outstanding 1974 seasons, and the confidence that underperformers like Munson and Chambliss could rebound from off years and meet their full potential, the stage appeared to be set for a return to the postseason for the century's greatest team in 1975.

It didn't happen.

The trouble began even before the start of spring training as Lou Piniella suffered an ear infection while playing winter ball in Puerto Rico, resulting in debilitating vertigo. The illness basically cost him his entire season and his batting average had dropped over one hundred points from the prior year when he finally submitted to season-ending surgery to correct the issue. The team stumbled out of the gate and played below .500 baseball until early June. This was followed by their best stretch of the season, as they won fifteen out of eighteen games and rose to the top of the standings before losing nine out of ten games. Still, they limped into the Fourth of July in strong contention. A dismal July all but knocked them out of the pennant race. The causes of the poor performance were many. Jim Mason's batting average dropped by a whopping one hundred points, Alomar provided almost no production at second base, and virtually every Yankee outfielder suffered injuries, most coming in the form of leg injuries caused or worsened by playing in the swampy Shea Stadium outfield. The low point came on a wet Friday evening in mid-June when Elliott Maddox, who was following his sensational breakout season of

1974 with an even more impressive performance in 1975, slipped in the wet Shea turf and injured his knee. With Bonds and Roy White already out of the lineup with injuries, Maddox tried to remain in the game. He slipped again a few plays later, and the resulting damage to his knee ended his season and essentially ruined his career. With their outfield ranks depleted, the Yankees were forced to field rookie Kerry Dineen in center field flanked by catchers Thurman Munson and Rick Dempsey in left and right field. This arrangement proved disastrous – Dempsey was no outfielder and Munson was even worse, and both Dineen and Dempsey joined the ranks of walking wounded with hamstring pulls. Bill Sudakis was not available with a "Band on the Run" style rallying cry – the utility man had been shipped to California in an off-season deal following his role in the fight in Milwaukee at the end of the prior season. While the Yankees struggled to field a healthy team, the Boston Red Sox emerged as a powerhouse and buried the Yankees in the standings. The Yankee front office, including Gabe Paul and the suspended George Steinbrenner, grew impatient and that impatience boiled over on August 2.

It seemed inevitable that Billy Martin would one day assume the role of Yankee manager. A disciple of mentor Casey Stengel, Martin had long coveted the Yankee managerial job. The fiery Martin had already cemented two elements of his managerial reputation that would remain with him for the rest of his life – he seemed to have a gift for turning around struggling ball clubs while being equally adept at wearing out his welcome by engaging in bizarre behavior both on and off the field. Martin had begun his major league managerial career in 1969 by leading a previously underachieving Minnesota Twins team to a divisional title in his first and only season as skipper of the team. A midseason incident that saw a drunk Martin beat one of his ace pitchers to a pulp was the most public of many infractions that resulted in his firing at the end of his successful freshman season. Two years later he was back in the saddle as manager of the struggling Detroit Tigers. Following a pattern that would continue throughout his managerial career, he drove the Tigers to an impressive second place finish in 1971 and a wholly unexpected divisional championship in 1972. Also following a pattern, the team's performance declined in 1973 and Martin's penchant for crazy behavior and outrageous stunts once again cost him his job, with Tiger general manager Jim Campbell noting that Martin "did a good job between the foul lines" but his off-the-field behavior was intolerable. Still, he was not out of work for long as the Texas Rangers hired him within days of his sacking in Detroit. Martin led the 1974 Rangers to the best finish in their history, but repeated his pattern of self-destruction and again found himself on the receiving end of a dismissal midway through the 1975 season. A mere day after Ranger owner Brad Corbett told Martin he was one misstep away from being fired and that he had better straighten himself out, the self-destructive Martin decided to force a showdown with the owner over what song should be played on the public address system during the seventh inning stretch. For Corbett this was the final straw and Martin's stay in Texas was over. Martin's ouster as manager of the Rangers triggered immediate action in the Yankee front office. Bill Virdon never overcame the second choice stigma in the eyes of Yankee brass, his Manager of the Year status notwithstanding. Despite Martin's well documented history of unstable behavior, the Yankees were convinced that he was the one person who could possibly breathe life into their dying pennant hopes. Martin's impatient, fiery, and most importantly, hands-on style appealed tremendously to George Steinbrenner and stood as the antithesis of Virdon. And so it was that reigning Manager of the Year Bill Virdon was unceremoniously fired on August 2, 1975. In a wonderful coincidence, Yankee prodigal son Billy Martin's triumphant return as manager would fall on the team's annual Old Timers' Day, with many of his former teammates on hand to witness his first game as the team's skipper.

The start of the Billy Martin Era did not yield any magical results. The team rallied to win six of eight under Martin, but ended up limping to a third place finish, twelve games behind the Red Sox. Despite the extreme difference in managerial styles, the record of the 1975 Yankees under Bill Virdon in the first half of the season and Billy Martin in the second half were virtually identical. The team would need more than a new manager to complete the climb back to the postseason. And this time there would be a twelve game gap to close.

Birthright Restored

In comparison to the dark days of the CBS era, Yankee fans generally had cause for optimism as a result of their club's off season efforts to improve the roster and build a championship contender. The arrival of the energetic Steinbrenner and his commitment to shake up the Yankee world had ignited a resurgence of confidence in 1973. The team's unexpected contention and the narrow loss to Baltimore in 1974 had been followed by the acquisition of two players who were arguably among the top performers in the game, a harbinger of great things for 1975. The fact that each of the three preceding seasons had ended with bitter disappointment did not dampen the hopes and dreams of Yankee fans as the 1975-76 Hot Stove League heated up. Chris Chambliss and Thurman Munson had rebounded from sub-par seasons in 1974 to form the core of a solid batting order, and the roster still featured a very deep starting pitching staff. There were holes to fill, but the Yankees now had a deeper roster of productive stars and promising minor leaguers and the possibilities for beneficial trades seemed better than ever.

The team's approach to player moves was made more complicated by the presence of the very opinionated and very vindictive Billy Martin. Bill Virdon did not enjoy the privileges of having a huge say in player moves, but Martin was never one to be shy about who he wanted, or more importantly, who he did NOT want on HIS team. Martin's unpleasant history with some of the Yankee players dated back to his previous managerial stops, and a number of players had targets on their backs from the day Martin arrived in New York. Others quickly joined their colleagues on Martin's enemies list. Alex Johnson, Larry Gura and Elliott

Maddox had all run afoul of Martin in Texas, but Gura and Maddox were now established players who had become local heroes during the team's 1974 pennant chase. Still, Gura was shipped off to Kansas City in early 1976 without appearing in a single game during the first six weeks of the season. It was widely speculated that Gura's spring training tennis playing and his other unorthodox (though obviously effective) personal training habits had once again appalled Martin to the point where Gura's Yankee tennis partner, Rich Coggins, was also dealt away at the same time as Gura after starting only a single game. Martin's unbridled animosity for Gura carried on even after the lefty settled into life with the Royals. New York and Kansas City newspapers reported numerous sarcastic and nasty quotes attributed to Martin regarding Gura, which Martin wrote off as gamesmanship. Gura also found himself the target of sharply personal bench jockeying by his former manager during postseason performances against the Yankees.

The Elliott Maddox situation was a bit more complicated for Martin. Since extricating himself from Martin's clutches in Texas, Maddox had become a star and under normal circumstances would have been at least slightly insulated from harassment from his manager. Unfortunately for Maddox, his 1975 knee injury kept him away from the club once Martin joined the team in 1975 and that same injury sidelined him for much of the 1976 season. The Yankees left Maddox exposed to the 1977 expansion draft and when he was not selected by either of the two new franchises he was eventually traded to Baltimore. Alex Johnson, another player who left Martin's Texas Rangers under a cloud, started just one game after Martin's arrival in New York and was released a few weeks later.

The disposal of players like Johnson, Gura, Coggins, and Maddox were merely a sideshow to the much more critical task of raising the talent level of the ball club. The Yankees made their first move in the rebuilding effort in late November, sending Pat Dobson to Cleveland in exchange for slugger Oscar Gamble. Dobson's performance had declined after his nineteen win season in 1974, and the outspoken pitcher was definitely not Billy Martin's type of guy. The team would be returning to the newly remodeled Yankee Stadium for the 1976 season, and Gamble's swing was tailor-made for the renovated Stadium's short right field porch. The team enjoyed one of the most consequential trading days in its Hot Stove history a couple of weeks later on December 11. On that day the team traded Doc Medich, Dobson's fellow pitching ace from the 1974 season, to the Pittsburgh Pirates for a three player package that included highly coveted rookie second baseman Willie Randolph. The acquisition of Randolph gave the Yankees a second baseman with the potential to be the highest impact player at that position since the retirement of Bobbie Richardson a decade earlier. Accompanying Randolph were pitcher Dock Ellis, slated to replace Medich in the starting rotation, and Ken Brett, who would be traded shortly after the season began to the White Sox for designated hitter Carlos May, filling another important gap in the lineup. The acquisition of Randolph was a coup of the highest order as the young man was possibly the most sought after ballplayer on the market. On that same day the Yankees flipped Bobby Bonds to the California Angels in return for outfielder Mickey Rivers and pitcher Ed Figueroa. Billy Martin always placed a high premium on speed, and Rivers was the reigning American League base stealing champion. The combination of speedy newcomers Randolph and Rivers fit perfectly into Martin's high intensity running game. As an added bonus, the acquisition of Figueroa gave the Yankees a quality starter who could very nicely fill the gap left by the departure of Dobson. With Lou Piniella fully recovered from his equilibrium issues and the hopes for continued success by Catfish Hunter, Thurman Munson, Sparky Lyle, Graig Nettles, and Chris Chambliss, Yankee fans rightfully hoped for final redemption and a return to the World Series. After a brief spring lockout by the major league owners over a labor dispute, the 1976 season opened with the Yankees winning ten of their first thirteen games, a start good enough to enable the club to end the month of April in first place. Although the level of competition in the American League east was fierce, Billy Martin's Yankees rolled through the 1976 season virtually unchallenged at the top of the standings. A midseason trade of Rudy May, Rick Dempsey, and highly coveted youngsters Tippy Martinez, Dave Pagan, and Scott McGregor (the latter once considered the "jewel of the franchise" and a prominent name in the failed negotiations over compensation for the signing of Dick Williams three seasons earlier) to the Orioles in exchange for veterans Ken Holtzman, Elrod Hendricks, Doyle Alexander, and Grant Jackson was emblematic of the new Yankee policy to trade young talent for veteran players. None of the players received from the Orioles would deliver any value to the Yankees after the 1976 season, while Dempsey and McGregor would star for Oriole teams for years to come. The "win now at all cost" mentality of George Steinbrenner, at first cheered by Yankee fans, would soon become a focal point for passionate debate among Yankee fans and media pundits. It was also as far from Lee MacPhail's policy of patient development of local talent in lieu of aggressive trading tactics as one could get. The club attempted to seal their pennant prospects by purchasing Vida Blue from

Oakland the same day as the Baltimore trade. A's owner Charlie Finley recognized that he was going to lose several stars to the newly negotiated free agent process following the 1976 season so he resolved to sell some of his top talent in order to raise the cash necessary to compete under the upcoming economic model. Finley's desire for George Steinbrenner's cash offset his deep antipathy for dealing with the Yankees, a resentment that had been further fueled by the Dick Williams incident and the subsequent Yankee signing of Catfish Hunter. Baseball Commissioner Bowie Kuhn put the kibosh on the sale of Blue to the Yankees as well as the sale of two other stars by Finley to the rival Red Sox, using his power to declare that the outright sale of players to the highest bidder created an unfair situation that favored team owners with large bank accounts over less fortunate teams, a situation deemed contrary to the best interests of baseball. In light of the 1920 sale of Babe Ruth to the Yankees by the Red Sox for $100,000 and without any other player compensation, this decision was thick with irony. In the end it was of no immediate consequence as the Yankees, minus Vida Blue, won the American League eastern division title by 10 1/2 games. It was the largest margin of victory in the division since the glory days of the Baltimore Orioles from 1969-1971.

The Yankees followed their successful 1976 regular season campaign by winning the League Championship Series with Kansas City in dramatic fashion. In the bottom of the ninth inning of the deciding fifth game, Yankee first baseman Chris Chambliss led off with a walk off home run. It was ironic that Chambliss, himself a prime example of the changing nature of the Yankee roster and the subject of an unfairly cool reception from his new teammates and from Yankee fans, would go down in history as the man who brought the Yankees back to where they belonged as if by birthright – to the World Series.

The euphoria of the victory over Kansas City quickly wore off as the Yankees faced Cincinnati's Big Red Machine in the 1976 World Series. The Reds easily swept the Yankees, leaving shocked Yankees fans with a mixed set of emotions over the 1976 season. Once again, George Steinbrenner stepped in with his checkbook to rekindle optimism for the following season. The winter of 1976-1977 brought with it modern baseball free agency, and the Boss finally had the opportunity to remove the bridles that had restricted the flexing of his financial muscle. Steinbrenner was naturally among the most aggressive owners in courting newly available stars, illustrated by the signing of marquee free agents Reggie Jackson and Don Gullett. The advent of free agency helped usher in a new era of Yankee dominance, beginning with back-to-back world championships in 1977 and 1978. The Yankees were indeed back where their fans felt they belonged.

The return of the Bronx Bombers to their familiar role as American League and world champions generated a fair amount of criticism focused on the influence of George Steinbrenner's considerable fortune and his willingness to spend lavishly to buy a winner. Accusations of having purchased a championship would follow the club and would continue to haunt the franchise throughout the rest of the twentieth century. To write off the rebuilding of the Yankees from the shambles inherited by the Cleveland Yankees in 1973 to the champions of 1976 as a purely economic exercise would be a serious mistake. True,

Yankee Resurrection

Steinbrenner's millions had netted Catfish Hunter, but the remainder of the club had been assembled by an aggressive pursuit of more traditional means. Of the twenty-eight most prominent members of the 1976 American League championship team, a mere five had come through the Yankee farm system, and only one of these (Thurman Munson) had been taken in the amateur draft. Only one player (Hunter) had been acquired by winning a free agent bidding war. The other twenty-two players, almost 80% of the total 1976 roster, were acquired either via small scale cash purchases or trades.

Player	Method of Acquisition
Doyle Alexander	Trade - Baltimore Orioles
Sandy Alomar	Purchased - California Angels
Chris Chambliss	Trade - Cleveland Indians
Rick Dempsey	Trade - Minnesota Twins
Dock Ellis	Trade - Pittsburgh Pirates
Ed Figueroa	Trade - California Angels
Oscar Gamble	Trade - Cleveland Indians
Fran Healy	Trade - Kansas City Royals
Elrod Hendricks	Trade - Baltimore Orioles
Ken Holtzman	Trade - Baltimore Orioles
Catfish Hunter	Free Agent
Grant Jackson	Trade - Baltimore Orioles
Sparky Lyle	Trade - Boston Red Sox
Elliott Maddox	Purchased - Texas Rangers
Tippy Martinez	Yankee Farm System - Amateur Signee
Jim Mason	Purchased - Texas Rangers
Carlos May	Trade - Chicago White Sox
Rudy May	Purchased - California Angels
Thurman Munson	Yankee Farm System - Amateur Draft
Graig Nettles	Trade - Cleveland Indians
Dave Pagan	Yankee Farm System - Amateur Signee

Lou Piniella	Trade - Kansas City Royals
Willie Randolph	Trade - Pittsburgh Pirates
Mickey Rivers	Trade - California Angels
Fred Stanley	Trade - San Diego Padres
Dick Tidrow	Trade - Cleveland Indians
Otto Velez	Yankee Farm System - Amateur Signee
Roy White	Yankee Farm System - Amateur Signee

So which method of building a championship team was the "right" way? Gabe Paul's Dial-a-Deal approach had yielded unquestionably good results. The disaster predicted by bitter players after four pitchers were dealt to the Indians in the April 1974 Friday Night Massacre did not develop. Chris Chambliss had emerged as one of the most productive bats in the Yankee lineup and Dick Tidrow had become an important counterpart to Sparky Lyle in the Yankee bullpen. Meanwhile, the four pitchers sent to Cleveland combined for a Wins Above Replacement score of -3 in the years following the trade, and by 1976 all but Tom Buskey were either out of the major leagues or were no longer effective pitchers. The trades that delivered Randolph, Ellis, Rivers, Figueroa, Piniella, Nettles, and other key contributors transformed the ball club.

Still, there was something to be said for Lee MacPhail's patient, steady development of in house talent, a tactic that had yielded Thurman Munson, Roy White, and much of the talent eventually traded for the imported stars – in order to get something of value in a trade, you need to give something of value.

And finally there was the Steinbrenner method – use cash to get immediate value without draining the roster. Elliott Maddox, Sandy Alomar, Rudy May, and the biggest catch of all, Catfish Hunter, were all products of George Steinbrenner's willingness to invest in a winning team.

The decline of the Yankee dynasty of 1921-1964 was the product of a number of factors, not one of which could be tagged as THE reason why the club stopped winning American League pennants and tumbled into mediocrity. By that same token, no single tactic could be elevated as the defining cause for the franchise's return to glory. Money, patience, and shrewd trading all contributed to the final outcome, but all had a common thread – an unbridled desire to break from the doldrums of insignificance and build a winning team. The 1974 Yankees set the stage, demonstrating how a group of capable players could come together, have fun, play confidently, and cast off the specter of losing that had plagued their predecessors, along the way answering that lingering question – yes, it is great to win, and it is even better if that winning team is a fun, exciting, and likeable group of professionals.

Epilogue

Bobby Murcer would spend two years in right field for the San Francisco Giants, rebounding from his disappointing final season with the Yankees by earning a spot in his fifth straight All-Star game during his first season on the west coast. It would be his last All-Star appearance. The Hall of Fame career predicted for Murcer did not come to fruition. His two seasons with the Giants were followed by a trade to the Chicago Cubs prior to the 1977 season. In his first year in the "friendly confines" of Wrigley Field, the thirty-one year-old Murcer hit twenty-seven home runs, the second highest total of his career. Murcer experienced a dream come true in June of 1979 as the Cubs traded him back to his beloved Yankees as his former club struggled to revive their rapidly fading pennant hopes. Murcer's jubilation over his return home was short-lived. Less than two months after the M&M boys were reunited, Thurman Munson was killed in a plane crash near his Ohio home. Murcer delivered one of the eulogies at his friend's funeral, then drove in the winning run in the emotional, come-from-behind victory that same night. Murcer's destiny to play in a World Series for the Yankees was fulfilled two years later as the aging veteran went hitless with a sacrifice bunt to his credit in four pinch hitting appearances in the 1981 World Series. Murcer's .091 overall batting average in postseason play, coupled with a career .077 batting average in five All-Star games, did little to diminish his standing in the eyes of Yankee fans. Murcer played his last game in 1983, retiring in June to move to the broadcast booth and clear a spot for rookie Don Mattingly after appearing in only a handful of games. Apart from a brief stint in the Yankee front office, Murcer cemented his place in the hearts of Yankee fans as a popular member of their broadcast team until his death in 2008.

The Yankee Stadium that Bobby Murcer returned to was much different than the one he left in 1973. The renovation conducted from 1974-1975 left the old ballpark something of a close replica of itself. The "death valley" of left center field, the super-short right field porch, the façade, and the monuments all remained, though all were changed in either dimension, location, or substance. As nice as the clean new shell looked, there was no denying that it hid a decaying framework. George Steinbrenner continued to lobby for a completely new stadium, but had made little progress toward that goal as the 1998 season began. A few hours before the start of a game on April 13, 1998, a massive steel beam crashed down from the upper deck into seats at the loge level. The stadium was closed for emergency safety inspections for ten days. Although the team was already scheduled for a road trip during most of that period, there was a need to fit in a home date against the west coast Anaheim Angels. In the absence of another viable contingency, on April 15 the New York Yankees returned to Shea Stadium as the home team twenty-three years after completing their second and final "home" season in Flushing. That single game against the Angels was the only game played under those circumstances at Shea as the building inspectors cleared Yankee Stadium for use shortly thereafter. The old ballpark remained in use for another ten years before being replaced by a new Yankee Stadium across the street from the original.

Lou Piniella was the last member of the 1974 Yankees to wear the pinstripes as a player. The popular outfielder who started the 1974 season as a stranger to Yankee fans and a man without a job remained with the team until 1984. The forty year-old Piniella, limited to a part-time role and plagued by a torn rotator cuff, still managed to hit .302 in his final season. Piniella would go on to hold several roles under George Steinbrenner, including two stints as Yankee manager. Sweet Lou went on to a long and successful career as a manager for Cincinnati, Seattle, Tampa Bay, and the Chicago Cubs. He went on to be one of the winningest managers in baseball history, leading the 1990 Reds to a world championship.

Lou Piniella's nemesis, Earl Weaver, remained one step ahead of his former player well after the two of them left the game. Weaver was honored with induction into the Hall of Fame in 1996, and despite a managerial career that featured more wins, more postseason appearances, and the same number of world titles (one) as his former skipper, as of this writing Lou Piniella has come painfully short of joining Weaver in Cooperstown. Dick Williams, who accrued one more world title as a manager than Piniella, but like Weaver had fewer total postseason appearances and many fewer wins than Piniella, joined Weaver in the Hall of Fame in 2008. Ralph Houk, whose managerial record was virtually identical to Williams, is not in the Hall of Fame and is rarely even mentioned as a candidate.

The George Steinbrenner era ended with the death of the Boss on July 13, 2010. During his time as Yankee owner the club won seven world championships and an additional four American League championships. Along the way two new dynastic eras came and went – the happy days of the return to glory from 1976-1981 and a stretch from 1996-2003 that was reminiscent of the great Yankee teams of the 1950s and 1960s. The era presented Yankee fans with a surreal mixture of on-the-field success punctuated by years of controversial personnel decisions that resulted in frustrating failure. The years 1982-1993 in particular made some Yankee fans pine for the blissfully lackadaisical days of 1965-1975. A revolving door of managers was highlighted by Steinbrenner's schizophrenic relationship with Billy Martin. From 1975-1988 Steinbrenner hired and fired Martin five times. It took the death of Martin in a 1989 car accident to prevent him from a probable sixth run as the team's manager. Steinbrenner's inexplicable obsession with future Hall of Fame outfielder Dave Winfield resulted in shady activities that earned the owner a second suspension. That dark period rivaled the CBS years as an era that most Yankee fans would like to forget, a period that combined the worst attributes of the owner with poor performance on the field. The resurrection and relative stability that coincided with the Joe Torre / Core Four era finally delivered the blissful combination that answered the prayers of the Yankee faithful – a brilliant collection of likeable player talent without the circus-like atmosphere forged by a headline hungry owner.

The callers to that Art Rust Jr. radio program so many years before would undoubtedly be pleased with that outcome.

The 1974 Yankees in Numbers

Batting Statistics

Batting Statistics	G	AB	R	H	2B	3B	HR	RBI	SB	CS	BA
Bobby Murcer	156	606	69	166	25	4	10	88	14	5	.274
Graig Nettles	155	566	74	139	21	1	22	75	1	0	.246
Lou Piniella	140	518	71	158	26	0	9	70	1	8	.305
Thurman Munson	144	517	64	135	19	2	13	60	2	0	.261
Roy White	136	473	68	130	19	8	7	43	15	6	.275
Elliott Maddox	137	466	75	141	26	2	3	45	6	5	.303
Jim Mason	152	440	41	110	18	6	5	37	1	2	.250
Chris Chambliss	110	400	38	97	16	3	6	43	0	0	.243
Sandy Alomar	76	279	35	75	8	0	1	27	6	4	.269
Ron Blomberg	90	264	39	82	11	2	10	48	2	1	.311
Bill Sudakis	89	259	26	60	8	0	7	39	0	0	.232
Gene Michael	81	177	19	46	9	0	0	13	0	0	.260
Fernando Gonzalez	51	121	11	26	5	1	1	7	0	0	.215
Rick Dempsey	43	109	12	26	3	0	2	12	1	0	.239
Otto Velez	27	67	9	14	1	1	2	10	0	0	.209
Mike Hegan	18	53	3	12	2	0	2	9	1	1	.226
Walt Williams	43	53	5	6	0	0	0	3	1	0	.113
Horace Clarke	24	47	3	11	1	0	0	1	1	0	.234
Fred Stanley	33	38	2	7	0	0	0	3	1	2	.184
Alex Johnson	10	28	3	6	1	0	1	2	0	0	.214
Jim Ray Hart	10	19	1	1	0	0	0	0	0	0	.053
Duke Sims	5	15	1	2	1	0	0	2	0	0	.133
Terry Whitfield	2	5	0	1	0	0	0	0	0	0	.200
Jim Deidel	2	2	0	0	0	0	0	0	0	0	.000
Larry Murray	6	1	1	0	0	0	0	0	0	1	.000

Pitching Statistics

	W	L	ERA	G	GS	CG	SH	SV	IP	SO
Pat Dobson	19	15	3.07	39	39	12	2	0	281	157
Doc Medich	19	15	3.60	38	38	17	4	0	279	154
Dick Tidrow	11	9	3.87	33	25	5	0	1	190	100
Rudy May	8	4	2.28	17	15	8	2	0	114	90
Sparky Lyle	9	3	1.66	66	0	0	0	15	114	89
Mel Stottlemyre	6	7	3.58	16	15	6	0	0	113	40
Cecil Upshaw	1	5	3.02	36	0	0	0	6	59	27
Larry Gura	5	1	2.41	8	8	4	2	0	56	17
Mike Wallace	6	0	2.41	23	1	0	0	0	52	34
Dave Pagan	1	3	5.11	16	6	1	0	0	49	39
Sam McDowell	1	6	4.69	13	7	0	0	0	48	33
Dick Woodson	1	2	5.79	8	3	0	0	0	28	12
Steve Kline	2	2	3.46	4	4	0	0	0	26	6
Tippy Martinez	0	0	4.26	10	0	0	0	0	12	10
Fred Beene	0	0	2.70	6	0	0	0	1	10	10
Fritz Peterson	0	0	4.70	3	1	0	0	0	7	5
Ken Wright	0	0	3.18	3	0	0	0	0	5	2
Tom Buskey	0	1	6.35	4	0	0	0	1	5	3
Rick Sawyer	0	0	16.20	1	0	0	0	0	1	1

Record Against Opponents

Opponent	Wins	Losses
Baltimore Orioles	7	11
Boston Red Sox	7	11
California Angels	9	3
Chicago White Sox	8	4
Cleveland Indians	11	7
Detroit Tigers	7	11
Kansas City Royals	8	4
Milwaukee Brewers	9	9
Minnesota Twins	8	4
Oakland Athletics	7	5
Texas Rangers	8	4

Record by Month, Home and Away

		Total			Home			Away	
	Won	Lost	PCT	Won	Lost	PCT	Won	Lost	PCT
APR	13	10	.565	9	4	.692	4	6	.400
MAY	10	17	.370	5	8	.385	5	9	.357
JUN	12	12	.500	5	6	.455	7	6	.538
JUL	16	13	.552	8	4	.667	8	9	.471
AUG	18	10	.643	11	4	.733	7	6	.538
SEP	19	10	.655	9	8	.529	10	2	.833
OCT	1	1	.500	0	0	.000	1	1	.500

Bibliography

There are a number of excellent books that address different aspects of the period described in this story of the 1974 Yankees. In addition to being an excellent source of research, they each do a wonderful job in telling related stories of the New York Yankee ball clubs of the periods referenced within this book.

Appel, Marty (2009). *Munson: The Life and Death of a Yankee Captain.* Diversion Books:New York.

Appel, Marty (2001). *Now Pitching For the Yankees: Spinning the News for Mickey, Billy, and George.* Diversion Books:New York.

Appel, Marty (2001). *Pinstripe Empire: The New York Yankees from Before The Babe to After The Boss.* Bloomsbury:New York.

Bashe, Philip (1994). *Dog Days: The New York Yankees' Fall from Grace and Return to Glory, 1964-1976.* Random House:New York.

Burke, Michael (1984). *Outrageous Good Fortune.* Little, Brown and Company:Toronto.

Goldman, Steve (Editor) (2007). *It Ain't Over 'Til It's Over: The Baseball Prospectus Pennant Race Book.* Basic Books:Philadelphia

Lally, Dick (1985). *Pinstriped Summers: Memories of Yankee Seasons Past.* Arbor House:New York.

Madden, Bill (2003). *Pride of October: What it Was to Be Young and a Yankee.* Warner Books:New York.

Murcer, Bobby with Waggoner, Glen (2008). *Yankee for Life: My 40-*

Bibliography

Year Journey in Pinstripes. HarperCollins:New York.

Pennington, Bill (2015). *Billy Martin: Baseball's Flawed Genius.* Houghlin Mifflin Harcourt:Boston, New York.

Peterson, Fritz (2014). *When the Yankees Were on the Fritz: Revisiting the "Horace Clark Era."* Fritz Peterson.

Piniella, Lou with Madden, Bill (2017). *Lou: Fifty Years of Kicking Dirt, Playing Hard, and Winning Big in the Sweet Spot of Baseball.* HarperCollins:New York.

Stottlemyre, Mel with Harper, John (2007). *Pride and Pinstripes: The Yankees, Mets, and Surviving Life's Challenges.* HarperCollins:New York.

White, Roy and Berger, Darrell (2009). *"Then Roy Said to Mickey…": The Best Yankee Stories Ever Told.* Triumph Books:Chicago.